CHILDCRAFT
THE HOW AND WHY LIBRARY

HOW DOES IT HAPPEN?

World Book, Inc.
a Scott Fetzer company
Chicago

Childcraft—The How and Why Library

CHILDCRAFT, CHILDCRAFT—THE HOW AND WHY LIBRARY, HOW AND WHY, WORLD BOOK and the GLOBE DEVICE are registered trademarks or trademarks of World Book, Inc.

World Book, Inc.
233 N. Michigan Avenue
Chicago, IL 60601

The Library of Congress has cataloged a previous edition of this title as follows.

Childcraft: the how and why library.
    v. cm.
    Summary: Presents illustrated articles, stories, and poems, grouped thematically in fifteen volumes.
    Includes bibliographical references and indexes.
    Contents: v. 1. Poems and rhymes -- v. 2. Once upon a time -- v. 3. Art around us -- v. 4. The world of animals -- v. 5 The world of plants -- v. 6. Our earth -- v. 7. The universe -- v. 8. How does it happen? -- v. 9. How things work -- v. 10. Shapes and numbers -- v. 11. About you -- v. 12. Who we are -- v. 13. See the world -- v. 14. Celebrate! -- v. 15. Guide and index.
    ISBN 0-7166-2203-3 (set)
    1. Children's encyclopedias and dictionaries.
[1. Encyclopedias and dictionaries.]
I. Title: Childcraft. II. World Book, Inc.
AG6 .C48 2004
031--dc21   2003008722

This edition:

ISBN-13: 978-0-7166-2219-2 (set)
ISBN-10: 0-7166-2219-X (set)
ISBN-13: 978-0-7166-2227-7 (Volume 8, How Does It Happen?)
ISBN-10: 0-7166-2227-0 (Volume 8, How Does It Happen?)

Printed in China
4 5 6 7 8 9 09 08 07 06

For information on other World Book publications, visit our Web site at **http://www.worldbook.com**, or call **1-800 WORLDBK (967-5325)**.
For information on sales to schools and libraries, call **1-800-975-3250 (United States), or 1-800-837-5365 (Canada).**

Contents

Introduction

We live in a busy world where something is always happening. In this book, you will find answers to a question you may ask many times each day, *How Does It Happen?*

People use machines to make things happen and to do work. For example, a simple machine made with a wheel and rope can be used to lift a bucket of water out of a deep well. A more complicated machine, such as a computer, can help people do math, writing, and other tasks that are part of their jobs or schoolwork. Machines of all kinds help us move things, put things together, take them apart, solve problems, and have fun.

In this book you'll learn about what makes machines work. The pulley depends on human energy, or movement, to work. Computers need energy from electric power to work. Energy can also come from the wind or the sun, from burning fuel such as wood or gasoline, or from the movement of tiny bits called atoms.

You'll also learn how heat is created, how white light breaks up into colors, and how sound travels. When you grow up, you could become a scientist and get a job studying the kinds of things you can read about in this book.

There are many features in this book to help you find your way through it. You'll find fun-filled facts in the boxes marked **Know It All!** You can amaze your friends with what you learn!

The book also has many activities that you can do at home. Look for the words **Try This!** over a colored ball. The activity that follows offers a way to learn more about how things happen. For example, you can make a paper helicopter to test how air affects moving things, create your own magnet, or change substances from one form to another.

Each activity has a number in its colored ball. Activities with a 1 in a green ball are simplest to do. Those with a 2 in a yellow ball may require a little

Know It All! boxes have fun-filled facts.

Each activity has a number. The higher the number, the more adult help you may need.

An activity that has this colorful border is a little more complex than one without the border.

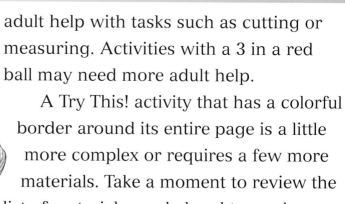

adult help with tasks such as cutting or measuring. Activities with a 3 in a red ball may need more adult help.

A Try This! activity that has a colorful border around its entire page is a little more complex or requires a few more materials. Take a moment to review the list of materials needed and to read through the step-by-step instructions before you begin.

As you read this book, you will see that some words are printed in bold type, **like this.** These are words that might be new to you. You can find the meanings and pronunciations of these words in the **Glossary** at the back of the book. Turn to the **Index** to look up page numbers of subjects that interest you the most.

If you enjoy learning how things happen, find out more in other resources, such as those listed below. Check them out at a bookstore or at your local or school library.

📖 **Day Light, Night Light: Where Light Comes From,** by Franklyn M. Branley, 1998. *In picture-book format, this well-known science author for children explains what light is and where it comes from.*

📖 **Energy,** by John Woodruff, 1998. *Step-by-step directions are given for 20 science experiments that can be done at home to gain an understanding of energy. See also,* Forces and Motion, *and* Sound and Electricity *in this "Science Project" series.*

📖 **Let's Investigate Science: Heat and Cold,** by Peter Lafferty, 1996. *Children learn how a toaster works and much more as they read and try the experiments in this book.*

📖 **The Magic School Bus and the Electric Field Trip,** by Joanna Cole and Bruce Degen, 1999. *Ms. Frizzle and her class have another adventure on their school bus—this time to learn how a power plant makes electricity.*

📖 **Ramps and Wedges,** by Angela Royston, 2003. *Simple pictures and easy text help explain what ramps and wedges do. From the "Machine Action" series.*

💿 **Science Blaster, Jr.,** CD-ROM for Mac and Windows, Davidson, 1997. *Explore the Blaster Ship's high-tech, fun-filled lab and participate in experiments as you discover the wonders of science.*

📖 **See and Explore Library: Machines and How They Work,** by David Burnie, 1991. *Read about machines of the past and see how they led to our modern machines.*

📖 **Sounds All Around,** by Wendy Pfeffer, 1999. *In picture-book format, this book explains how sounds are made and includes some sound activities.*

📖 **What Makes a Magnet,** by Franklyn M. Branley, 1996. *This "Let's-Read-and-Find-Out Science" book explains the properties of magnets and features experiments to help you understand magnets.*

📖 **What Makes a Shadow,** by Clyde Robert Bulla, 1994. *Shadows are fascinating. This picture book explains what makes a shadow.*

What Happens with Machines?

Machines can be any shape and size, but they all have one thing in common: they help people do work. When we think of machines, we usually think of big ones with many parts. These machines do big jobs, such as digging holes, washing clothes, or mowing lawns.

But some machines are small. You cut things out with a small machine—a pair of scissors. You sew with a small machine—a needle. And you tighten a screw with a small machine—a screwdriver. These small machines help you do work, too.

A Lever Is Clever

How many times can you lift your best friend higher than your head? How many times can your best friend lift you? It doesn't sound easy, but it is. When you and your friend are on a seesaw, that's exactly what you are doing.

The seesaw you and your friend are riding is really a kind of machine called a **lever** (LEHV uhr). A lever makes pushing and lifting easy, even when things are hard to move.

The simplest kind of lever is just a straight stick or board and something to rest it on. Suppose you want to move something heavy—a big rock for example. You can push one end of a strong board under the rock. Then you can rest the middle of the board on a log. This is the resting place, or **fulcrum** (FUHL kruhm). The end of the board near you sticks up. If you push down on the high end of the board, the other end will move up. The heavy rock will move, too.

A lever rests on a fulcrum. The thing you lift is attached to the lever.

When you push one end of the lever down, the other end rises. It lifts the thing you want to move.

Seesaws are levers.

KNOW It All!

Archimedes (AHR kuh MEE deez), an ancient Greek scientist, was the first person to describe how levers work. To prove the power of levers, he built a machine that he used to launch a ship all by himself.

When you ride a seesaw, you and your friend take turns using it as a lever. The middle of the seesaw is the fulcrum. Your weight pushes one end down and lifts your friend up. Then your friend's weight pushes the other end down and lifts you up.

Make an Alligator Long-Arm

Levers make it easier to lift big, heavy things. They can also help you pick up things you can't quite reach. This alligator long-arm uses pairs of levers to make other levers move.

You Will Need:

corrugated cardboard
a ruler
a pencil
scissors
7 paper fasteners
green and white
　　construction paper
glue

What To Do:

1. Use the ruler and pencil to mark out six strips of corrugated cardboard. Each strip should be about 6 1/2 inches (16.5 centimeters) long and 3/4 inch (2 centimeters) wide. Leave a "tooth" on two of the strips, as shown.

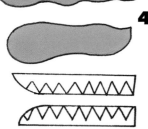

2. Cut out the strips. Then use the pencil to punch a hole in the middle of each one.

3. Fasten together the pairs of strips without teeth to make two X shapes.

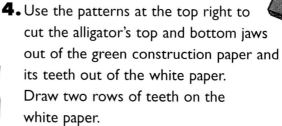

4. Use the patterns at the top right to cut the alligator's top and bottom jaws out of the green construction paper and its teeth out of the white paper. Draw two rows of teeth on the white paper.

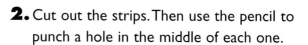

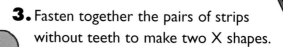

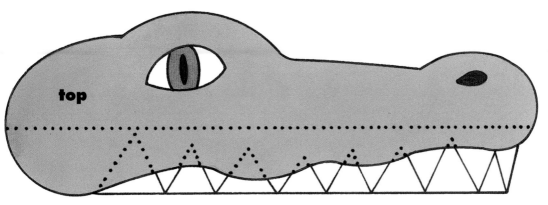

5. Glue the teeth onto the alligator's top and bottom jaws along the dotted line as shown. Draw in the eyes and nose.

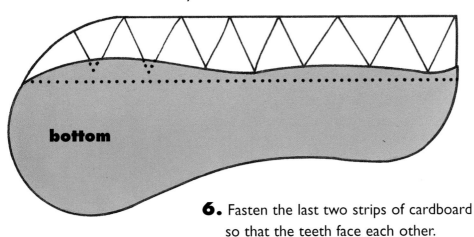

6. Fasten the last two strips of cardboard so that the teeth face each other.

7. Glue the alligator's bottom jaw onto the bottom cardboard strip. Glue the alligator's top jaw to the other cardboard strip.

8. Line up the cardboard X shapes as shown at the upper left and punch the rest of the holes. Fasten the shapes together.

Your alligator long-arm works like a pair of scissors. When you close the handles together, the end with teeth closes, too. You and your friends can take turns using the long-arm to pick up small cardboard fish or "pirate treasure." See who can make the biggest catch!

Slides and Steps

Is a slanted board without a fulcrum a machine? It is if you use it to do some work. It is a kind of simple machine called an **inclined plane** (ihn KLYND playn). *Inclined* means slanted, and a plane is a flat surface. So an inclined plane is a flat surface that slants, like a slide on a playground.

An inclined plane makes it easy to move things up and down. When you use an inclined plane, you spread out the amount of work you do. If you lift a heavy box onto a table, you move it only a short distance—straight up. But you are doing all the lifting at once. If you slide the box up an inclined plane, you do the lifting little by little, so the job is easier.

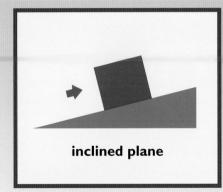

inclined plane

There are other ways to use inclined planes, too. When you wheel your bike or roll a wheelchair up and down a ramp, you are using an inclined plane.

The kind of inclined plane you use most often may not look like one. A stairway is an inclined plane with steps on it. The steps help keep the plane shorter. Imagine how long the inclined plane would have to be if you flattened out the stairs!

An inclined plane makes it easier to slide a load upward than to lift it directly. The longer the slope is, the smaller the effort is needed.

A Shape That Splits

Be careful! That knife is sharp! Don't stick yourself with that pushpin! Working with sharp things means taking special care. But some things have to be sharp to work well. A dull knife or a pushpin without a point isn't much help at all.

Sharp things have a special shape that makes work easier. They are really all one kind of machine—a machine called a **wedge** (wehj). The thin, sharp end of a wedge can cut or push into things easily. Then the thicker part of the wedge can push through. Knives, saws, and scissors are wedges for cutting. Pushpins, nails, and needles are wedges used for pushing into or through things. The point makes it easy for the pushpin to stick into a bulletin board, for the nail to push into wood, and for the needle to push through cloth.

knife

Sharp things are wedges that can cut through objects.

saw

16

Axes and metal wedges are used to push the sharp edge into a log. Then the wider part spreads the wood and makes it split.

Many boats have a wedge-shaped bow, or front end. The bow cuts through the water and makes it easy for the boat to glide along.

A boat with a wedge-shaped bow can cut smoothly through the water.

When struck with a mallet, a wedge can split wood.

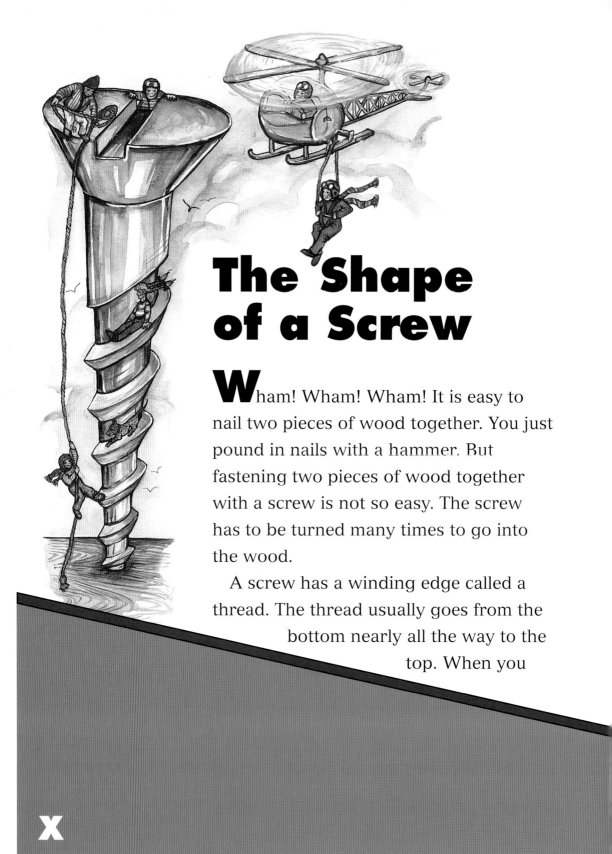

The Shape of a Screw

Wham! Wham! Wham! It is easy to nail two pieces of wood together. You just pound in nails with a hammer. But fastening two pieces of wood together with a screw is not so easy. The screw has to be turned many times to go into the wood.

A screw has a winding edge called a thread. The thread usually goes from the bottom nearly all the way to the top. When you

X

turn the screw, you wind the thread into the wood.

Turning a screw takes more time than pounding in a nail the same size. But the winding thread of the screw is much longer than the straight sides of the nail. There is more of it to grip and hold the wood. So for some jobs, a screw works better than a nail. It holds things together better than nails.

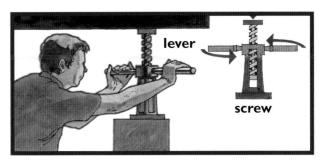

lever

screw

A screw is an inclined plane that curves around. A jack uses a lever and screw. It can lift a heavy load.

TRY THIS! 2

A screw really is an inclined plane that curves around and around. Make a paper screw and see for yourself. Cut a triangle shape as shown from a corner of construction paper. Mark the square corner with an X.

The long cut edge is an inclined plane. Color this edge with a crayon or marker. Starting at the straight end, with the X next to the eraser, wind the triangle around a pencil. The colored edge shows you how the inclined plane winds around the screw to form the threads.

Wheels and Axles

Four wheels, two axles (AKS uhlz), a box, and a handle. That is all a wagon is. But with a wagon, you can easily carry a couple of friends or even give your dog a ride.

When you use a wagon, wheels and **axles** are helping you. You can see the wheels. They are the round parts that roll over the ground. The axles are the rods that connect each pair of wheels. The wheels and axles turn together.

A wagon rolls along on wheels and axles.

Putting wheels and axles on something makes it easier to move. It would be hard to pull a wagon without wheels. It would just drag over the ground. But wheels on axles roll along smoothly. Cars, trucks, and buses have wheel-and-axle parts, too.

Every day you are helped by other kinds of wheels—wheels that do not roll. A doorknob is a kind of wheel-and-axle machine. The knob is the wheel! You turn it to make the axle pull back the latch so the door can open.

A pencil sharpener has a wheel and axle, too. The handle is part of a wheel. When you turn the handle, it turns an axle that makes the other parts work.

Ups and Downs

Suppose someone asked you to lift a hippopotamus! It sounds impossible, but with a simple machine called a **pulley** (PUL ee), you could do it.

A pulley is a special kind of wheel and axle. A rope or steel cable fits around the rim of the wheel. When one end of the rope is pulled down, the rope slides over the wheel, which turns on the axle. Then the load at the other end moves up.

With one pulley, the load moves up as far as you pull the rope down. You work just as hard to pull the rope as you would to pick up the load, but you can pull in a direction that is easier for you.

With two pulleys, you can make lifting even easier. The second pulley is attached to the thing you lift. Each part of the rope between the pulleys holds half the weight, so you pull only half as hard to move the load. But the load is held up by twice as much rope. So you will have to pull the rope twice as far as the distance you want the load to move.

The more pulleys you use, the easier it is to lift a load. But you will have to pull

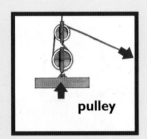

pulley

When the cable is pulled, it glides over the wheels of the pulley and lifts the load.

more and more rope. You might be able to lift that hippopotamus with a hundred pulleys, but you will have to pull a lot of rope!

Your hippopotamus lifter has two types of pulleys—fixed and movable. The fixed pulleys are attached to the beam. They stay in one place while the load moves. The movable pulleys are attached to the hippo.

KNOW It All!

Wheels with Teeth

Why should a wheel have teeth? Wheels don't eat. But some wheels use teeth to help them do work, work that other wheels can't do.

A wheel with teeth is called a **gear**. It is a wheel that makes other wheels move. If you look at an eggbeater, you can see three gears. The big one with the handle is the gear you turn. The teeth on this gear fit into the spaces between the teeth on the two smaller gears. When you turn the handle, the teeth on the big gear push against the teeth on the small gears and make these gears turn. One turn of the big gear makes the small gears turn many times. So the beater blades move very quickly.

First, second, third, fourth—these are the different-sized gears that fit together in a car. The engine turns a set of

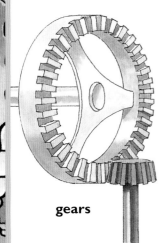

gears

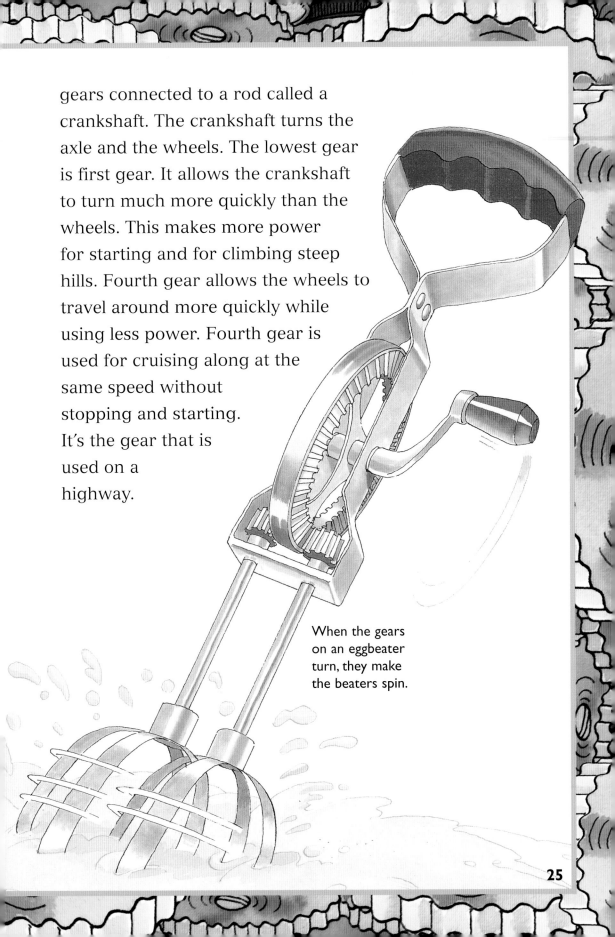

gears connected to a rod called a crankshaft. The crankshaft turns the axle and the wheels. The lowest gear is first gear. It allows the crankshaft to turn much more quickly than the wheels. This makes more power for starting and for climbing steep hills. Fourth gear allows the wheels to travel around more quickly while using less power. Fourth gear is used for cruising along at the same speed without stopping and starting. It's the gear that is used on a highway.

When the gears on an eggbeater turn, they make the beaters spin.

The Amazing Machine Show

TRY THIS!
1

The people in the picture are all using different kinds of machines. Can you find the machine that each riddle below is describing?
See the answers on the bottom of page 27.

1. Wheels and axles make me go.
 I use a wedge to scrape up snow.

2. I'm pretty clever—I dig with a lever.
 My teeth are wedges with pointed edges.

3. With a screw and handle, I'm strong. I'll prove it.
 I can lift a house if you want me to move it.

4. Moving wedges with very sharp edges,
 Will help you prune and trim your hedges.

5. Don't want to climb? Take a ride on me.
 I'm an inclined plane with steps, you see.

6. You'll find me where kids swing, climb, and run.
 I'm an inclined plane that you ride for fun.

7. Pulleys raise me to let in sun,
 Or lower me down when the day is done.

8. What are you riding? Wheels for the street—
 And small wheels with levers you work
 with your feet.

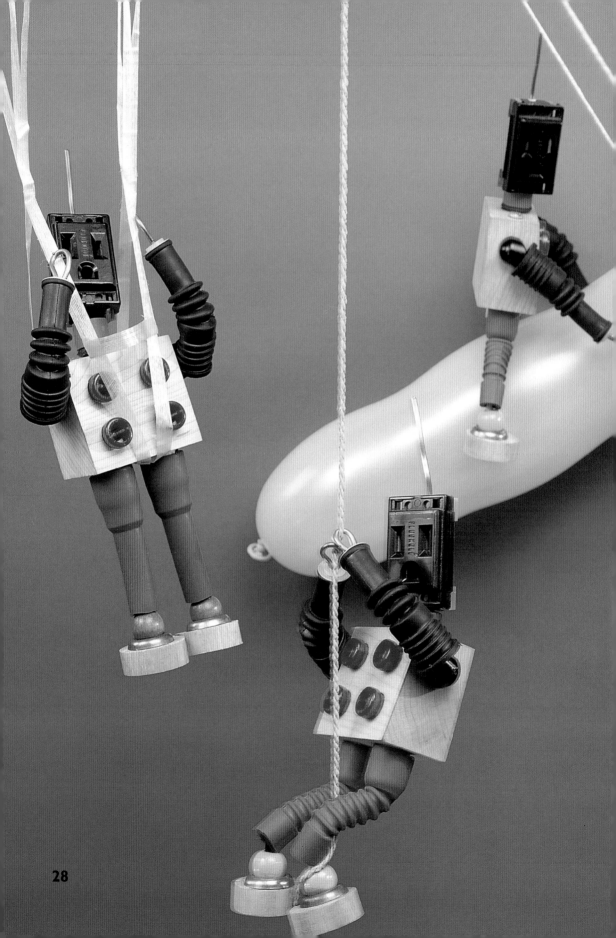

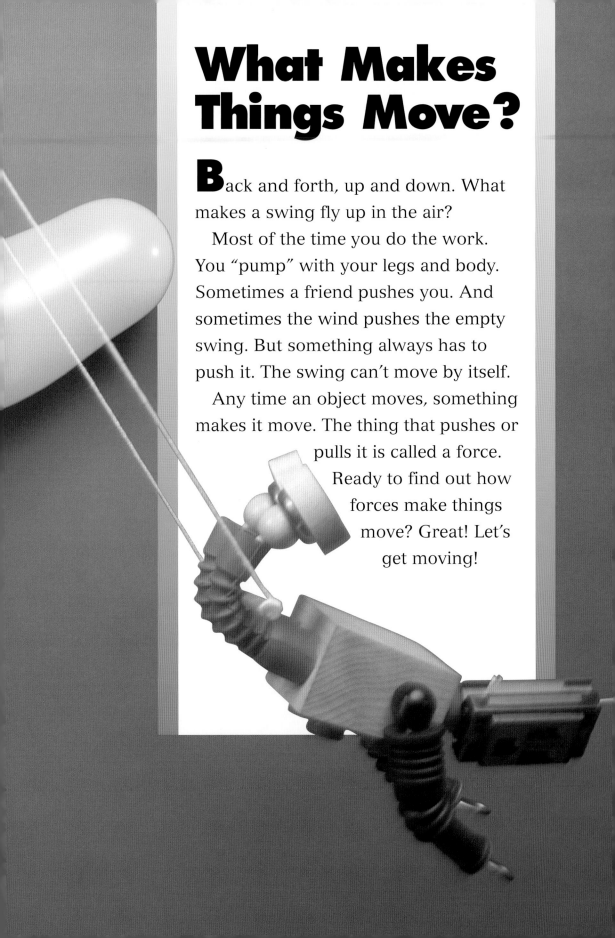

What Makes Things Move?

Back and forth, up and down. What makes a swing fly up in the air?

Most of the time you do the work. You "pump" with your legs and body. Sometimes a friend pushes you. And sometimes the wind pushes the empty swing. But something always has to push it. The swing can't move by itself.

Any time an object moves, something makes it move. The thing that pushes or pulls it is called a force. Ready to find out how forces make things move? Great! Let's get moving!

The Invisible Push

The light turns green, and the car starts to move quickly. You feel as if a big, invisible hand pushes you back in the car seat. When the car stops quickly, the same "hand" seems to push you forward.

What is this invisible "something" that pushes you when a car starts and stops? It's called **inertia** (ihn UHR shuh).

Inertia is the name for the way things resist a change in movement. When something is stopped, it stays stopped. It starts to move only when a force—a push or a pull—makes it move. And when something is moving, it tries to keep moving. It won't stop until a force stops it.

Use a whirling egg to see the force of inertia. Let a fresh egg warm up to room temperature. Then place the egg in a bowl. Gently spin the egg by batting it with your finger. Stop the egg from spinning by touching it lightly on the top. Then quickly lift your finger from the egg. What happens?

The egg starts spinning again. Why? When you start the egg spinning, the liquid inside the shell spins, too. When you stop the egg, inertia makes the liquid inside keep spinning. When you let go of the egg, the spinning liquid makes the egg start spinning again.

When a car starts to move, your body tries to stay stopped. So you feel yourself pressing back as the car seat moves forward. And when the car stops, your body tries to keep moving. Inertia "pushes" you forward. Your seat belt is there to hold you back.

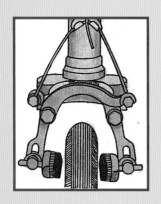

handlebar bicycle brake

A Force for Stopping

There's a big stick on the sidewalk. Slow down your bike! Then you can go around the stick safely.

Your bike has brakes to help it stop. When you squeeze the levers on the handlebars or push the pedals backward with your feet, the brakes rub against the wheels and stop them from turning. The rubbing that stops the wheels is called **friction** (FRIHK shuhn).

Friction happens because all things have a rough surface. Even things that look shiny and polished have very tiny areas that are not smooth. When one object slides across another, the rough spots rub against one another. This rubbing, or friction, makes things move more and more slowly, until finally they stop.

Friction is useful when it helps you stop

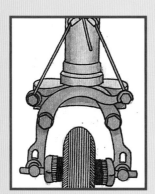

brake off   **brake on**

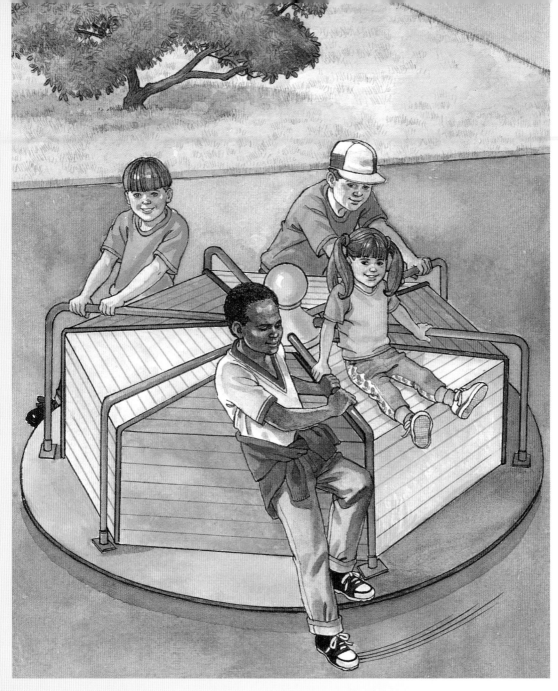

your bike. But sometimes we want things to keep moving smoothly. Then we need to lessen friction. We can do this with a slippery substance, such as oil or grease. For example, the grease on your bicycle chain lessens friction so that you can pedal easily and smoothly.

The friction of the boy's dragging foot stops the merry-go-round.

Friction from Air

Even air creates friction. It rubs against moving things and slows them down. You can make a helicopter that uses the friction of air to slow its fall—and to spin, too.

You Will Need:

letter-sized
   construction paper
a ruler
a pencil
scissors

What To Do:

1. Place the paper with the short edge facing you. Fold the paper in half lengthwise.

2. Open the paper. Fold the bottom corners until they meet at the center crease. You will have two folded triangles at the bottom of the paper.

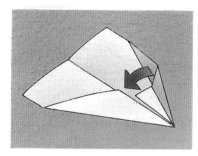

3. Fold the outer edge of each triangle in as far as the center crease. That's your helicopter.

4. Hold the helicopter with the point downward. Let it drop. Does it fall quickly or slowly? Here is something you can do to slow it down.

5. Measure 1 inch (2.5 centimeters) up from the center crease from where the folded edges meet. Make a mark.

6. Cut along the crease from the top down to the mark. Fold the paper forward on one side of the cut and backward on the other side to make two flaps.

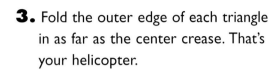

7. Now drop your helicopter again. This time it should fall more slowly, spinning as it goes. The friction of the air rubbing against the two flaps makes all the difference.

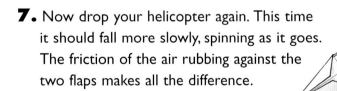

A Machine that Never Stops

Dr. Mothbold's automatic polka-dotting machine can paint polka dots on anything—shirts, socks, pancakes, and even pretzels!

Best of all, the polka-dotter is a **perpetual motion** (puhr PEHCH oo uhl MOH shuhn) machine. Perpetual motion is movement that goes on forever.

All the parts of the polka-dotter create forces that make the other parts work. As each part gets a push or pull, it gives a push or pull to another part. So, says Dr. Mothbold proudly, this machine will never stop! Is the doctor right?

No. Although pushes and pulls will keep the machine going for a while, other things will make it slow down. Friction is one of these things. The rubbing of wheels against the belt,

the brushes rubbing as they paint, and the bumping of the brushes on the paint **lever** will slow down the machine. Finally, the automatic polka-dotter will stop.

People have tried to make all kinds of perpetual motion machines. But the friction that slows the machines is always a little stronger than the forces the machines make to keep running. That is why perpetual motion does not work.

A Force that Pushes and Pulls

Magnets can do some strange things. That's what makes them such fun to play with. They can stick to each other. They can make nails or pins hang onto each other. They can even "lead" each other across a piece of glass. A magnet on top of the glass follows a magnet you slide along under the glass.

A special force, or pull, makes a magnet work. The pull is strongest in two places called poles— a north pole and a south pole.

horseshoe magnet

Both poles of a magnet will hang onto iron and steel things, like pans and pins. And either pole will hang onto one pole of another magnet. The north pole of one magnet and the south pole of the other will pull on each other, and the magnets will stick together like best friends.

bar magnet

But magnets stick together only if the poles don't match. If you put two north poles or two south poles together, the magnets try to push each other away!

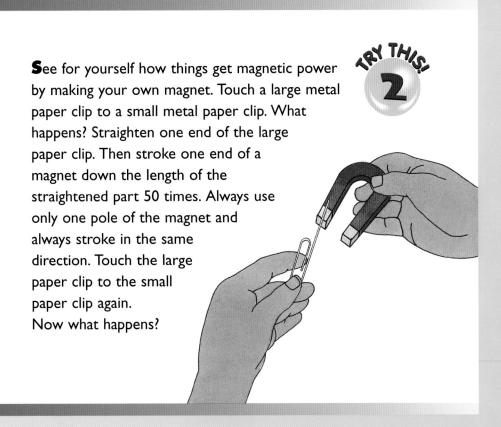

See for yourself how things get magnetic power by making your own magnet. Touch a large metal paper clip to a small metal paper clip. What happens? Straighten one end of the large paper clip. Then stroke one end of a magnet down the length of the straightened part 50 times. Always use only one pole of the magnet and always stroke in the same direction. Touch the large paper clip to the small paper clip again. Now what happens?

TRY THIS!
2

Canceling Pushes

Imagine a restaurant with a swinging door leading to the kitchen. Two servers try to push the door open from opposite sides at the same time. One holds a huge bowl of spaghetti. The other balances a tray of dishes. If they both push with the same force, the door doesn't move. But if the server with the spaghetti does not push as hard as the other server, the door swings open. And crash—spaghetti flies everywhere!

If two servers push on the door with the same force, the door is in equilibrium.

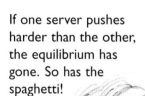

If one server pushes harder than the other, the equilibrium has gone. So has the spaghetti!

When equal forces push on an object from opposite sides, that object is in **equilibrium** (EE kwuh LIHB ree uhm). An object in equilibrium is balanced. It won't move or tip over unless an extra push is added from one direction.

A force called **gravity** (GRAV uh tee) pulls all objects downward, toward the center of the earth. Every object has its own center of gravity, the spot where it can be balanced. If you support an object at its center of gravity, it will be in equilibrium.

Ask a grown-up to help you carefully stick a small fork into a small potato, with the top side of the fork facing upward. Next, find a pencil that is longer than the fork.

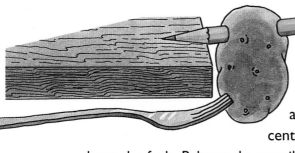

Push the pencil into the other side of the potato until about 1 inch (2.5 centimeters) sticks out above the fork. Balance the pencil tip on the edge of a table, with the fork extending below the table. The potato stays balanced because its center of gravity is actually in the pencil tip!

What Keeps Them Up?

How do an airplane's wings help it stay in the air? Airplane wings have a special shape. They are curved on top and straight on the bottom. This shape is what helps lift the plane up.

When the plane starts to move, the wings cut through the air. The air moves over the curved top of the wing and under the straight bottom. The air moving over each wing pushes down on it. And the air moving under each wing pushes up.

Since the curved top of the wing is longer than the straight bottom, air

How an airplane takes off

It speeds up.

Different wing shapes help airplanes fly in different ways. Planes that fly at both low speeds and high speeds have wings that stick straight out from the plane. Wings that sweep backward—like the wings of the Stealth plane shown here—help a plane to fly better at very high speeds.

moving above the wing travels farther than air moving below it. So air going above the wing moves faster. The faster it moves, the less it pushes. As the push over the wing gets weaker, the stronger push under the wing begins to lift the plane. So the plane leaves the ground. As long as the plane keeps moving forward, the wings lift it and help it to fly.

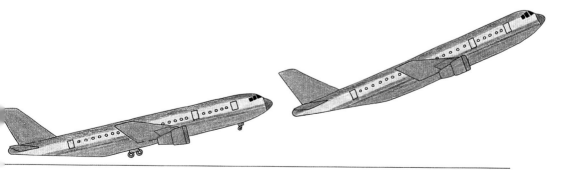

The air begins to push under the wings.   The airplane flies.

Satellite Flight

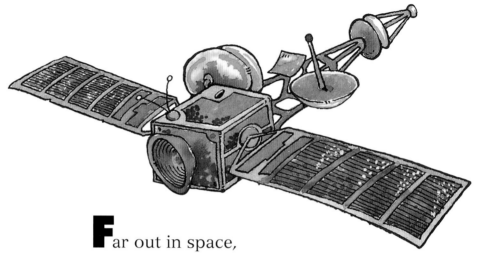

Far out in space,
a satellite circles the earth.
What keeps it from crashing into the
earth? And what keeps it from sailing
away into space?

Two kinds of forces work to make the
satellite circle the earth. One is the
tremendous push of the satellite's speed—
thousands of miles per hour. Without this
push, gravity would pull the satellite back
to the earth.

The other force is the pull of the earth's
gravity, which reaches far out into space.
Without this pull, a satellite would travel
in a straight line, away from the earth.

Gravity pulls the satellite toward the
earth. But the speed of the satellite

pushes it outward. When the push and the pull are even, the satellite can't sail away from the earth—or fall back to the earth, either. Instead, it speeds around the earth, making a circle in space.

A satellite pushes away from the earth. It tries to escape. But the earth's gravity pulls the satellite. It is captured and held in place as it circles around the earth.

This type of satellite circles the earth sending television or telephone signals from one place to another.

Falling in Space

Imagine floating through the air, or standing on the ceiling. An astronaut orbiting, or circling, the earth in a spacecraft can do both because of something called weightlessness.

Orbiting the earth is really a lot like falling in space. If you threw a stone from a very high mountain, it would curve down gently before it hit the ground. The harder you threw the stone, the farther it would go. The surface of the earth is curved. What if you could throw a stone so hard that the curve as it fell was exactly the same as the curve of the earth? The stone wouldn't hit the ground—it would go into orbit. In other words, it would become a satellite of the earth.

A spacecraft "falls" around the earth in the same way. This constant falling

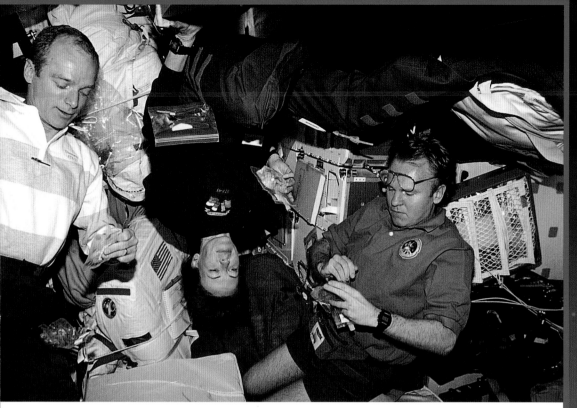

These astronauts are weightless in space. You can see this because the woman's hair and the man's glasses are floating. The astronauts float, too, unless they hold onto something.

makes everything inside the spacecraft seem like it has no weight at all.

What happens then? The astronauts float, unless they hang on to something! Anything they "drop" floats in the air when they let go of it. And if they jump, they don't come down. They hit their heads on the ceiling instead.

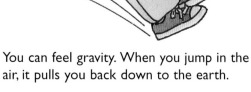

You can feel gravity. When you jump in the air, it pulls you back down to the earth.

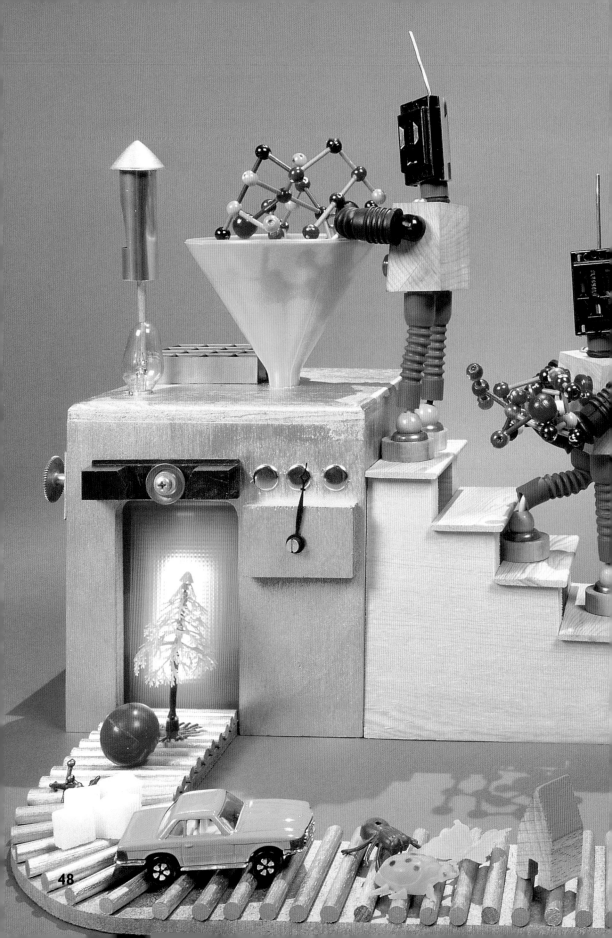

What Is Matter?

Everything is made of matter. Matter is anything that has weight and takes up space, so a rock, a dandelion, a rabbit, and a puddle of water are all matter. And you are matter, too. There is matter in everything around you.

Even air is matter. You don't feel how much air weighs because most things are heavier than air. But air has weight. And it takes up space. You feel it take up space when you breathe. You see it take up space when you blow up a balloon.

Bits and Pieces

What is in a sand castle? Millions and millions of tiny grains of sand. The many grains of sand are packed together to make a single shape, like a castle with towers, walls, and bridges.

In this pyrite (PY ryt), sometimes called fool's gold, you can see the smooth, flat surfaces of a crystal.

You can see the way atoms line themselves up by looking at crystals. Most matter that is not alive is made up of crystals. Crystals form when some kinds of atoms move together and join. When these atoms join, they form regular shapes. So crystals have sharp edges and smooth, flat surfaces. These surfaces are called crystal faces.

KNOW It All!

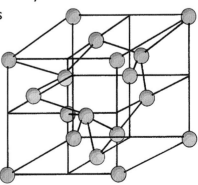

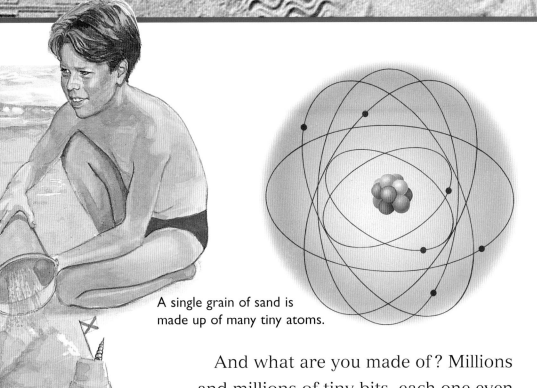

A single grain of sand is made up of many tiny atoms.

And what are you made of? Millions and millions of tiny bits, each one even smaller than a grain of sand. You and everything around you—people and animals, cars, rocks, water, and even the air—are made of tiny bits that are put together in different ways.

These bits are called **atoms** (AT uhmz). Atoms are much smaller than a grain of sand. In fact, they are so small that you can't see them. But if you could see them, you would find that these tiny atoms are made up of even smaller pieces.

Even though atoms are so small that you can't see them, they still have weight, and they take up space. They are tiny bits of matter. Everything that is matter— even you—is made up of tiny atoms.

Kinds of Matter

How many kinds of matter are there? So many that if you started to count them, you probably would never finish.

But if you could sort out the atoms in all that matter, you would find that there are only about 100 kinds. Each of those 100 kinds of atoms is a different size.

Some kinds of matter are made up of only one kind of atom. These kinds of matter are called **elements** (EHL uh muhnts).

copper
+
sulfur
?

copper

sulfur

Gold is an element. A piece of pure gold is made of just gold atoms. Iron is an element, too. It is made of just iron atoms.

gold

But most kinds of matter are made of two or more kinds of atoms joined together. These kinds of matter are called **compounds** (KAHM powndz).

iron

Water is a compound made of an element called oxygen (AHK suh juhn) and an element called hydrogen (HY druh juhn). By themselves, oxygen and hydrogen are invisible **gases**. You cannot see them. But when they join together, they make a liquid you can see and feel—water.

copper + sulfur = copper sulfide

The elements copper and sulfur are often found joined in nature. They form a compound, copper sulfide.

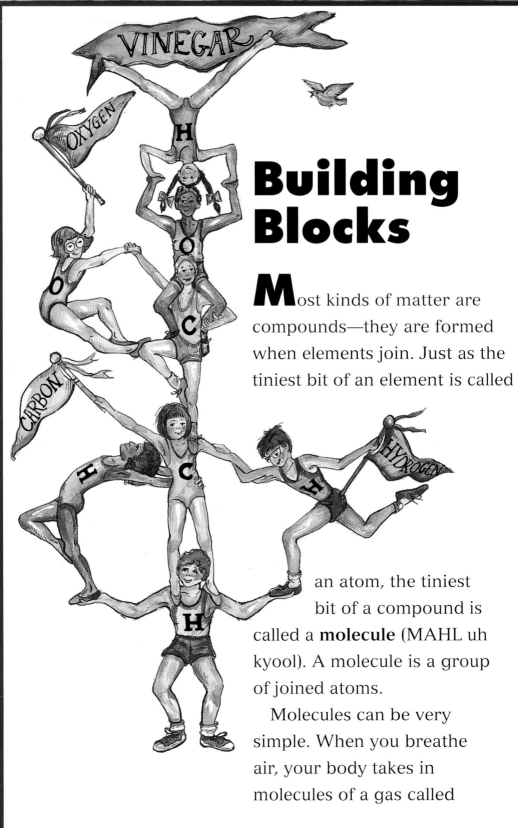

Building Blocks

Most kinds of matter are compounds—they are formed when elements join. Just as the tiniest bit of an element is called an atom, the tiniest bit of a compound is called a **molecule** (MAHL uh kyool). A molecule is a group of joined atoms.

Molecules can be very simple. When you breathe air, your body takes in molecules of a gas called oxygen. Each oxygen molecule is made up of two oxygen atoms joined together.

But some molecules have many kinds of atoms. The "vinegary" taste of vinegar comes from a molecule containing two carbon atoms, four hydrogen atoms, and two oxygen atoms. And some molecules are made of thousands of atoms. Bread and potatoes contain giant molecules that look like chains—the chains have thousands of molecules.

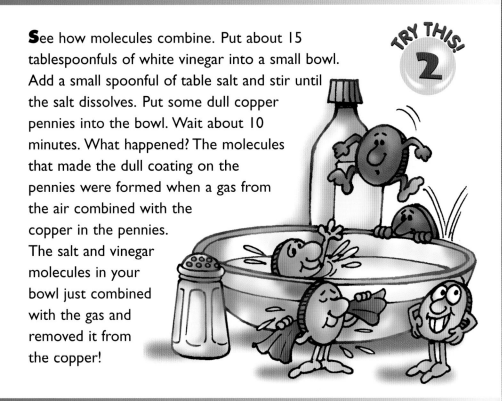

See how molecules combine. Put about 15 tablespoonfuls of white vinegar into a small bowl. Add a small spoonful of table salt and stir until the salt dissolves. Put some dull copper pennies into the bowl. Wait about 10 minutes. What happened? The molecules that made the dull coating on the pennies were formed when a gas from the air combined with the copper in the pennies. The salt and vinegar molecules in your bowl just combined with the gas and removed it from the copper!

TRY THIS!
2

The Signal from the Rock

It was the 1890's, and a young Polish-born scientist named Marie Sklodowska Curie hurried home through the streets of Paris. But her thoughts were back in the unheated, leaky shed where she worked. She was puzzled over an experiment she had done over and over. The result had been the same each time, but she could not explain why!

In this experiment, Marie used a rock called pitchblende that gave off mysterious rays of energy. These rays were like a signal, but the signals made no sense at all.

Marie believed that the signals from the rock might be coming from an element that no one knew about. So she began trying to find it. She boiled the pitchblende in huge pots. Next she added chemicals to it to break up the different compounds. Then she tested each part to see if it gave off rays. Her work took a long time, and many of her experiments went wrong.

Finally, Marie found the element that gave off the energy. She named it radium (RAY dee uhm). The radium gave off so much energy that it glowed in the dark! It took Marie four years and several thousand pounds of pitchblende to get just a tiny pinch of pure radium.

Marie's work was hard, but it paid off. In 1903, she won a Nobel Prize, the most important award in science—and she gave the world a new element.

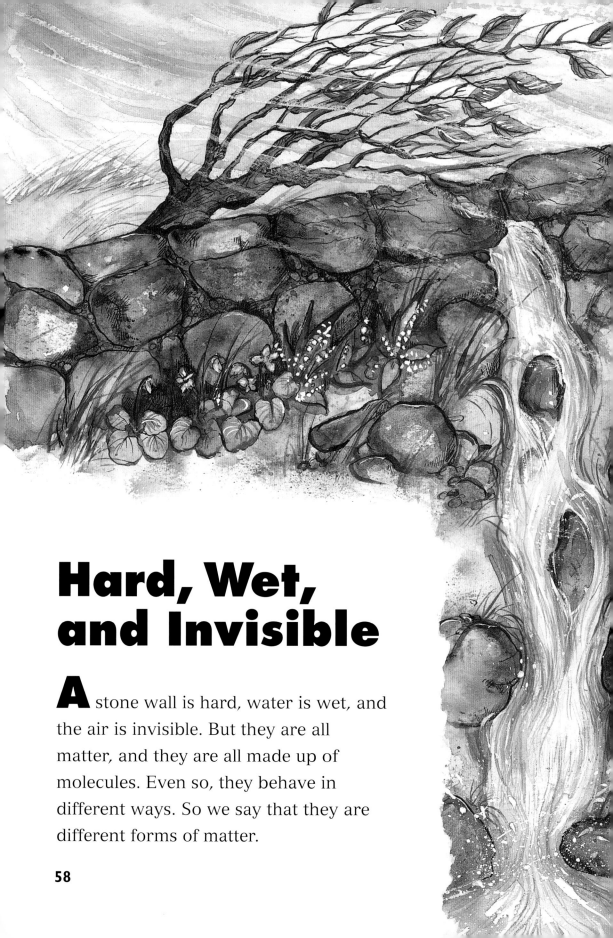

Hard, Wet, and Invisible

A stone wall is hard, water is wet, and the air is invisible. But they are all matter, and they are all made up of molecules. Even so, they behave in different ways. So we say that they are different forms of matter.

Stone is a **solid** (SAHL ihd). It has a shape of its own. The molecules in most solids are very close together. They pull hard on each other. This pull makes solids keep their shape.

Water is a **liquid** (LIHK wihd). It has no shape of its own. It takes the shape of the container it is in. Molecules in most liquids are farther apart than molecules in a solid. They don't pull as hard on one another. So the molecules of a liquid can slide around and take any shape.

Air is a gas. It has no shape of its own, either. Its molecules are so far apart that they hardly pull on one another at all. Molecules of a gas bounce around so easily that they can squeeze into a small balloon or spread out to fill a big room.

Mealtime Matter

TRY THIS!
1

Like everything else in the world, the foods and drinks we enjoy are made of matter. Like all matter, they can be in the form of solids, liquids, or gases. Many foods change from one form of matter to another when we change their temperature. See if you can match the foods and drinks listed in the boxes below and on page 62 with the numbered clues. See the answers on the bottom of page 63.

Foods

a.   **buttered toast**

b.   **cola**

c.   **soft-boiled egg**

d.   **spaghetti**

e.   **soup**

f.   **ice cream**

g.   **fried fish**

h.   **frozen orange juice**

i.   **salad**

Breakfast

1. I start out as a cold solid. After you stir me with a clear liquid, you can drink me.

2. I start out as a soft, flat solid. When you heat me, I turn crisp. I taste good when I'm spread with a yellow solid that melts.

3. I start out as a white solid filled with soft, gooey liquid. If you boil me for three minutes, part of me turns into a solid. You can draw a face on me before you crack me and eat me.

Foods

a. buttered toast
b. cola
c. soft-boiled egg
d. spaghetti
e. soup
f. ice cream
g. fried fish
h. frozen orange juice
i. salad

Lunch

4. I'm a cold liquid filled with tiny bubbles of gas.

5. I'm a liquid mixed with chunks of solids. You can eat me with a spoon or slurp me from a mug.

6. I'm chunks of solids dipped in thick liquid. Then I'm cooked in a hot liquid until I'm crispy and golden.

Dinner

7. I start out as thin, hard sticks. When you boil me in a liquid, I get soft. I taste delicious with a warm, red liquid poured over me.

8. I'm all different kinds of crunchy raw solids. You can toss me in a bowl with a bit of oily or creamy liquid.

9. I'm a sweet, frozen solid that you scoop out of a box.

Answers:
1. h; 2. a; 3. c; 4. b; 5. e;
6. g; 7. d; 8. i; 9. f.

What Is Energy?

Opening doors, playing baseball, running a race—you really keep moving. What gives you the power to move?

The answer is energy! Your body gets its energy from food. The energy you get makes the pushes and pulls that keep you moving.

A car engine burns gasoline. As the gasoline burns, it gives off energy. That energy makes the pushes and pulls that turn the wheels.

There are many kinds of energy. Things that move, such as water and wind, have energy. Things that burn, such as fire, have energy. But the most important source of energy is the sun. It keeps everything on the earth on the move.

387

65

Energy from Movement

Poor old Bristlebones! His pirate ship has sailed away, and he's stranded on a tiny island. He can think of only two ways to get help. He can fly a kite and hope somebody sees it. Or he can put a message in a bottle and let it float away in the ocean and hope somebody finds it.

Line up some dominoes as shown. Give one of the end dominoes energy by nudging it so that it tips over onto the domino next to it. Watch the energy pass from one domino to the next as they topple over.

TRY THIS!
1

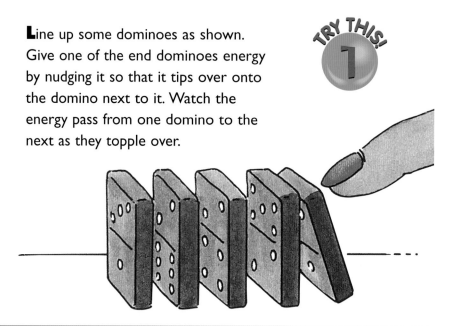

Each of old Bristlebones' ideas depends on a kind of **energy**—the movement of wind to lift a kite and the movement of water to carry a bottle. Moving things like wind and water have energy that can be used to give something else a push or a pull.

Anything that is moving has energy, even the coconuts on Bristlebones' tree. While the coconuts are falling, they can give quite a push to anything they hit, including Bristlebones' head!

Energy from the Wind

A push from the wind can make a kite fly. It can make a sailboat speed across the water. It can do other things, too. It can even light lamps and pump water.

People use wind energy to pump water and make **electricity** (ih lehk TRIHS uh tee) for their homes. They do it with the help of a machine called a windmill. Windmills come in different shapes and sizes, but they are all alike in some ways.

They are tall enough to catch the strong winds that blow high above the ground. They also have a wheel, which is the part that spins. The wheel has paddles, sails, or blades for the wind to push against. When the wind blows, the wheel spins. This makes a push that runs a water pump or an electricity-making machine called a **generator** (JEHN uh RAY tuhr).

Of course, the wind doesn't always blow, so the windmill doesn't always

These windmills use the energy of wind. The one in front pumps water, and the ones on the hill make electricity.

run. But water pumped by the windmill can be stored in tanks. And electricity made when the windmill runs can be stored in batteries. Until the windmill goes back to work, people can use stored-up water and stored-up electricity in their homes. There are even "wind farms," where many windmills make electricity for whole communities.

Energy from the Sun

Someday you may live in a house that keeps itself warm with a tankful of "sunshine." The heat for such a house comes from **solar** (SOH luhr) **energy**, or energy from the sun.

The sun's energy gives power to everything on the earth. Using the sun's energy, plants make food for animals and people.

A house that uses the sun's energy is a solar house—a "sunshine house." A solar house has special collectors to capture the sun's heat. Usually the collectors are on the roof or on the sunniest side of the house.

How is the sun's heat stored? In one kind of solar house, water or another liquid is pumped through collectors on sunny days to pick up heat. Next, the hot water is pumped to a huge tank filled with sand or gravel. Bit by bit, it heats the whole tank. Sand or gravel can hold heat longer than water does, so heat stays in the tank long after the sun goes down.

KNOW It All!

Solar cells are special batteries that can make electric power directly from sunlight. Solar cells work best in space because that is where sunlight is strongest. Many satellites get their power from solar cells.

When the house is chilly, you just press a button that turns on a fan beside the tank. The fan pulls the cool air into the hot tank. When the air gets warm, it blows out of the tank and through the house. So the house gets warm, and you do, too—with a tankful of stored-up heat from the sun.

A solar house

1. Solar panels collect the sun's heat.

2. Water is pumped through collectors to pick up heat.

3. Hot water carries heat to the storage tank.

4. Cool air is warmed in the hot tank and blown through the house.

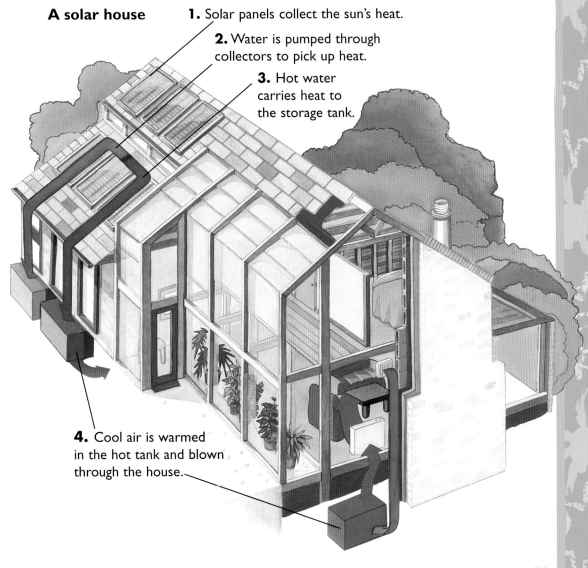

Energy from Burning

Candle wax is a fuel.

You have seen candles burning. An orange flame dances around the wick, while the wax melts underneath and drips down. The candle gets shorter as the wax melts.

The candle wax has a kind of stored-up energy. It is a **fuel**. A fuel is something that is burned to make light, heat, or a push that makes things move. The coal, oil, and gas used to heat homes and other buildings and to cook food are

a coal fire

fuels. The gasoline in a car and the wood in a fireplace are fuels, too.

The same thing happens to every kind of fuel when it burns. When it starts burning, the heat makes it break down and change to other things, such as ashes. As the fuel breaks down, it gives off energy. Some of the energy is light, and some is heat.

When gasoline is burned in a car engine, the heat energy makes the engine push. The push from the engine makes the car run.

The energy stored in a fuel is called **chemical** (KEHM uh kuhl) **energy**.

Energy from Atoms

All things—even you—are made up of billions and billions of "bits" that are smaller than anything you can imagine. These "bits" are called **atoms** (AT uhmz). Atoms are the tiniest parts that something can be broken into and still be the same stuff. For example, one atom of gold is the tiniest bit of gold possible.

Special machines can split certain kinds of atoms into even smaller parts. When atoms split, they give off energy.

How nuclear energy is made

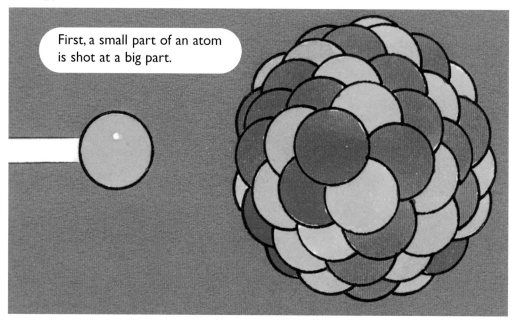

First, a small part of an atom is shot at a big part.

The part of the atom that splits is called the nucleus (NOO klee uhs), so the energy is called **nuclear energy**.

The energy given off by atoms when they are split is in the form of heat. So a machine that splits atoms can be used the same way a fuel-burning engine is used. The machine makes heat. The heat can be used to run generators that make electricity and to run other machines, too.

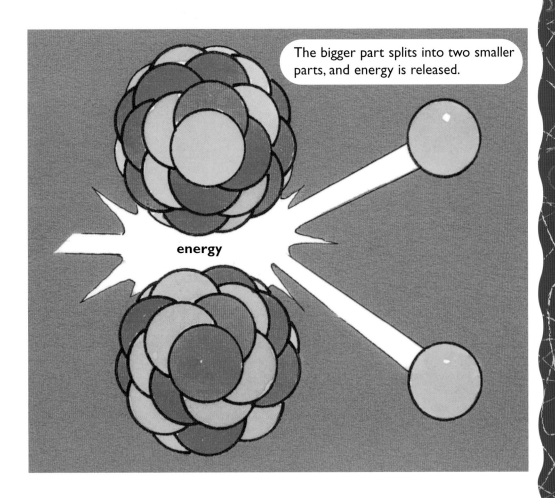

The bigger part splits into two smaller parts, and energy is released.

energy

Energy from Electricity

Snorkel and Scorch are terribly sad. For 200 years they worked as palace dragons. They carried wood for fires, huffed flames into fireplaces, and lit candles in the palace halls. But now they are out of work. It is not their fault. Things at the palace have changed. Now the royal halls are lit with light bulbs, and the rooms are heated with a furnace. There is even a brand-new stove in the kitchen.

Electricity is doing the work that Snorkel and Scorch used to do. Electricity makes one kind of energy. When electricity flows through a wire, much as water flows through a hose, it is

KNOW It All!

The word *electricity* comes from the Greek word *elektron*, which means "amber." Amber is a yellow stone that gets an electric charge when it is rubbed with a cloth. You can read all about this type of energy, called static electricity, in the chapter "What Happens with Electricity?"

called an electric **current** (KUHR uhnt). An electric current can do the same kind of work a fuel can do. It can make light and heat. And it can make the push or pull that runs a machine.

So Snorkel and Scorch do not have to carry wood, light fires, or keep the candles burning any more. All they have to do is push the switches that turn the electric current on and off. Life will be much easier from now on, and Snorkel and Scorch will have enough free time to help out at palace barbecues.

Changing Energy

Biff! The racket hits the tennis ball, and the ball sails across the net. A point is scored— thanks to a hamburger!

Of course, the hamburger did not actually hit the ball. The player did. But the player ate the hamburger for lunch, and the player's body got energy from the hamburger. Some of this energy was used to swing the racket. And the energy in the swinging racket knocked the ball over the net. So stand up and cheer for the hamburger. It helped score the point!

There are only a few kinds of energy. But each kind of energy can change into other kinds. Chemical energy in the food you eat can be changed into the energy of movement when you run or hit a ball.

Other Kinds of Energy

In some parts of the world, energy comes roaring up out of the ground or rolling across the ocean—for free!

One form of this energy is gathered from boiling water and **steam**. The rocks deep below the surface of the earth are very hot, sometimes as hot as 1100 °F (600 °C). This is about five times hotter than boiling water. If underground water trickles into these hot rocks, it turns into steam. The steam takes up about 4,000 times more room than the water. The steam forces its way into cracks in the rocks and sometimes finds its way to the surface. The steam can be piped into an electricity-making machine called a turbine (TUHR byn). The steam turns wheels of the turbine, which helps a generator make electricity.

Movement in the oceans also releases huge amounts of energy.

At this power station in New Zealand, boiling water and steam from deep underground are used to make electricity.

A turbine is an electricity-making machine that uses steam.

People have invented several ways to use this energy. One way uses the power of the rising and falling tides. To capture this energy, a dam is built across the opening to a bay. At high tide, the dam is closed to hold water in the bay. At low tide, the water can be released. The flowing water spins wheels inside a turbine to help make electricity.

What Makes It Work?

Find the kind of energy that makes each thing work.

1. A light bulb gets its energy from

    a. burning wood
    b. electricity
    c. sunlight

2. An automobile is powered by

    a. burning fuel
    b. wind
    c. wheel

3. When you eat, your body gets energy

    a. from the movement of your jaws when you chew
    b. from the food you eat
    c. from electrical energy in your stomach

4. A sailboat uses the energy that comes from

   a. light
   b. burning wood
   c. wind

5. A solar house gets energy from

   a. candles
   b. sunlight
   c. steam

6. When you bake a cake in the oven, you use

   a. heat energy
   b. the energy of moving things
   c. moving water

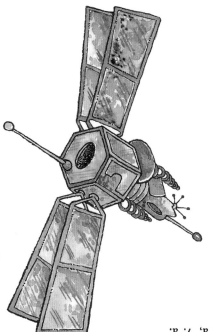

7. An orbiting satellite uses energy

   a. from the sun
   b. from water in the air
   c. from burning fuel

Make a Snake Dancer

You Will Need:

- a pencil
- tracing paper
- tape
- construction paper
- scissors
- a thimble
- an unsharpened pencil
  with eraser
- a spool
- a needle

Make this moving toy and you will see how heat energy can make something move.

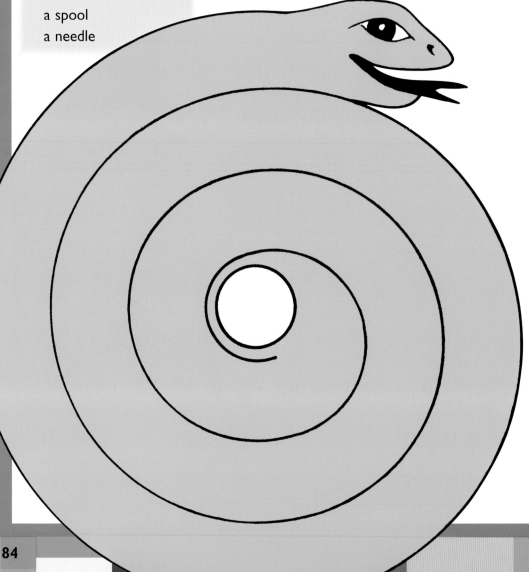

What To Do:

1. Trace the snake pattern shown here on the tracing paper. Tape the paper onto the construction paper.

2. Cut around the outside of the shape. Then carefully poke your scissors through the center and cut out the circle. The hole should be big enough to fit over the thimble. If it is not, make it bigger. Then cut along the spiral line.

3. Push the thimble into the hole. Gently pull on the snake's head to make the spiral open up.

4. Stand the pencil in the spool, with the eraser up. If the pencil wobbles, stuff paper in the hole. Have a grown-up help you poke the needle into the eraser. Hang the thimble over the needle, as shown here, to make the snake "stand."

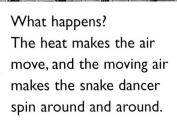

5. Put your snake dancer in a warm place—on a radiator, a fireplace mantel, or on top of a television set—or hold it over a lit light bulb.

What happens?
The heat makes the air move, and the moving air makes the snake dancer spin around and around.

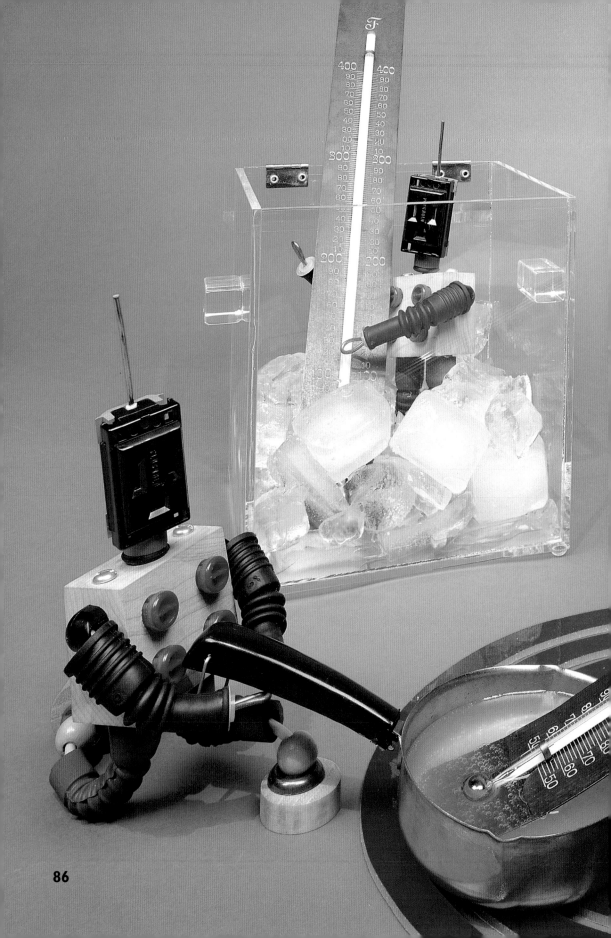

What Is Hot and Cold?

On a chilly day, you can rub your hands together to warm them. Why does rubbing your hands make them warm?

You are made up of molecules, just like all the other kinds of matter around you.

When you rub your hands together, you create friction. You make the molecules in your skin bump and push one another.

That makes the molecules speed up. It gives them more energy. The faster the molecules move, the warmer you get. So if you rub hard enough, your hands feel warm.

Heating Up

Can you fry ice cubes? You can try, but if you heat ice cubes in a pan, they won't be ice cubes anymore. The ice will melt into water. And after a while, the water will boil and turn into **steam.** What makes the ice cubes change?

Ice melts because something happens to its **molecules.** Heat **energy** makes the molecules move faster. As the molecules speed up,

Heat changes ice cubes from a solid (ice) to a liquid (water) and then to a gas (steam).

they begin to move away from one another. Then the ice changes from a **solid** to a **liquid**—water.

Heat speeds up the molecules in liquids, too. So as the molecules speed up, they move even farther apart. Finally, they lose almost all their pull on one another. Then the liquid **evaporates** (ih VAP uh rayts). It becomes a **gas.**

Cold molecules stay
close together.

And that's what happens when water boils. Heat makes the molecules roll and tumble faster and faster in the pan. When the water molecules are moving fast enough, they become steam. The molecules of steam mix with other molecules in the air.

Heat makes the molecules speed up
and move away from one another.

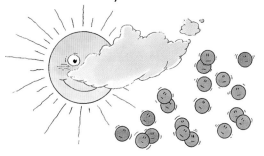

As molecules speed up, they lose their
pull on one another.

Beeeeep. . . . Your food is ready to come out of the microwave. How did it get warm? A microwave oven shoots waves of energy called microwaves (MY kroh wayvz) into the food. The microwaves make the molecules in the food vibrate. This vibration causes heat. Your food gets warm.

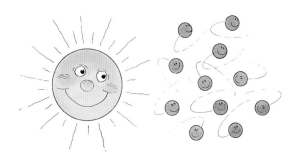

KNOW
It All!

Chilling Out

Sometimes, in cool weather, the insides of our windows look cloudy. They are covered with a thin film of water. Where does this water come from?

It comes from water vapor (VAY puhr), water molecules mixed with the air inside the house. The water collects on the windows when the glass is cool.

Water vapor is a gas. The molecules of water vapor are as warm as the air around them in the house, so they move very fast. But when the molecules hit the cool glass in the window, they lose heat. As the molecules grow cooler, they move

The molecules of water vapor are as warm as the air around them, so they move very fast.

closer together and slow down. When they are moving slowly enough, they **condense** (kuhn DEHNS), or turn into tiny drops of liquid.

Sometimes when the weather is very cold, the glass in the windows gets much colder than the air inside the house. Then the molecules of water vapor lose even more heat when they touch the glass. They slow down much more and move much closer together. When they get close enough to pull hard on one another, they freeze. Then the window is covered with frost— thin, feathery bits of solid ice.

How cold can things get? At the lowest temperature possible, molecules hardly move at all. This temperature is called absolute zero. Absolute zero is -459.67 °F (-273.15 °C) below zero.

KNOW It All!

As the air begins to cool, the water molecules slow down and move toward one another.

When the water molecules get close enough to pull hard on one another, they freeze.

Moving Molecules

Here is a way to show that molecules in hot water move faster than molecules in cold water.

You Will Need:

2 large bowls
cold water
hot water
food coloring

What To Do:

1. Fill one large bowl with the coldest water you can get. Have a grown-up help you fill the other large bowl with hot tap water. Put both bowls on a table.

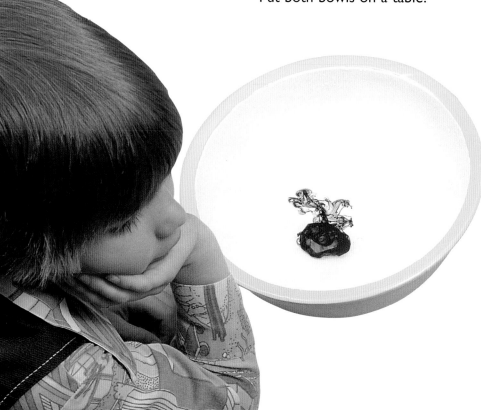

2. Wait until the water is still. Then squeeze three drops of food coloring into the center of each bowl. Don't touch the water as you do this. Do it quickly so that the drops go into both bowls at almost the same time.

How fast does the food coloring spread in each bowl? The molecules of hot water are moving faster than the molecules of cold water. So the food coloring spreads much faster in the bowl of hot water.

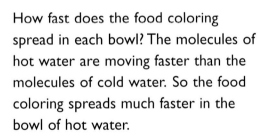

As Warm as Toast

Cold butter on hot toast doesn't stay cold for very long. Some of the heat from the toast passes into the butter, and so the butter becomes warm, too. The heat is a form of energy. Heat energy can spread. Heat energy always flows from something warmer to something cooler. The movement of molecules passes the heat along.

When you spread cold butter onto hot toast, some of the fast-moving toast molecules (red) bump into the slow-moving butter molecules (blue).

A slice of toast is a solid piece of bread. But the molecules in the bread move. They wriggle and jiggle, even though they are held together. As the bread is toasted, the heat from the toaster makes the molecules speed up.

Cold butter is solid, too. But its molecules are moving very slowly. When you spread the cold butter onto the hot

94

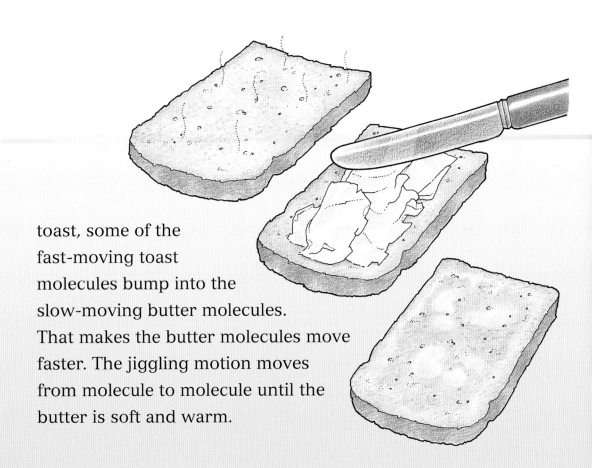

toast, some of the
fast-moving toast
molecules bump into the
slow-moving butter molecules.
That makes the butter molecules move
faster. The jiggling motion moves
from molecule to molecule until the
butter is soft and warm.

Put five coins with different dates in a small box.
Show them to some friends and explain that you
will read your friends' minds. While your back is
turned, have your friends choose one of the coins
and remember its date. Ask each friend to hold the
coin tightly in one hand for a moment and to
concentrate on the date. When everyone has
had a turn, have the last person drop the coin
in the box. Turn around right away and touch
each coin lightly. Four of the coins will be
cool—but the fifth will be warm, because it has
taken heat energy from your friends' hands. Pick
that coin, read the date, and amaze your friends!

TRY THIS!

1

Going Up!

Do you know that some people fly on a bag of hot air? Of course, the "bag" is a huge hot-air balloon. A balloon filled with hot air can lift people.

When air is heated, its molecules speed up and begin to push on one another. This makes the air expand, or take up more space. The molecules of hot air push farther and farther apart until only a few molecules take up a great deal of space.

The molecules of hot air that fill a balloon are farther apart than the molecules of colder air outside the balloon. So the hot air weighs much less than the colder air. Because the hot air is lighter, it rises. It pushes up inside the balloon. When the push is strong enough, it lifts the balloon high into the sky.

Ask a grown-up to heat a toaster. Standing a few feet away from the toaster, blow soap bubbles so that they float above it. Watch the bubbles rise as they reach the hot air above the toaster! Be careful not to get the toaster wet! Electricity and water are dangerous together!

TRY THIS!

What Makes a Pot Lid Bounce?

You don't have to watch a covered cooking pot to know when the food or water inside it is boiling. The lid will begin to bounce up and down when the water begins to boil. The push that moves the lid comes from steam.

As the water inside the pot is heated, the molecules take up energy. That energy makes the molecules speed up and push hard against one another. When the water is hot enough, some of it changes from a liquid to a gas called steam.

The molecules of gases move around more and are farther apart than the molecules of liquids. So the steam expands. It takes up much more space than the hot water did. But there is only one place where the steam can escape—through the spaces around the pot lid. It squeezes out with a hard push, and the push bounces the lid up and down.

Steam also can be used to push the moving parts of machines—to run ships, trains, and factories that make electricity. Such big machines need very strong pushes from expanding steam. So huge amounts of water must be boiled.

Making Changes

All around us, there are solids, liquids, and gases. So in everything around us, molecules behave in certain ways. They hang together tightly, slide around each other, or move about freely in space. By heating up or cooling down matter, it's easy to change matter from one form to another. These three activities and the observations on page 103 will show you how!

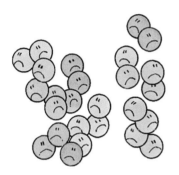

You Will Need:

3 glasses of the same size
2 ice cubes
cold butter
a coin
a metal pan
water
a metal jar lid big enough to fit
    over the glasses (If there is
    cardboard in the lid, remove it.)

What To Do:

Activity 1

Make sure the glasses are the same temperature as the room. Put an ice cube in the first glass, a small piece of butter in the second glass, and a coin in the third glass.

Now leave the glasses for 10 to 20 minutes.
Which of the three materials has melted?

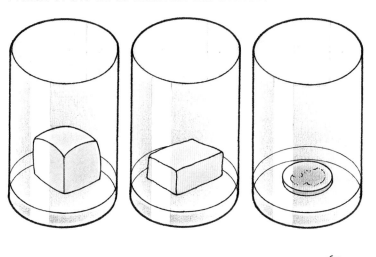

Activity 2

Have a grown-up help you pour
1 inch (2.5 centimeters) of hot
water from the tap into
the pan. Set the glasses
from Activity 1 in the
pan and leave them for
10 minutes. What
changes do you see
in the materials in
the glasses?

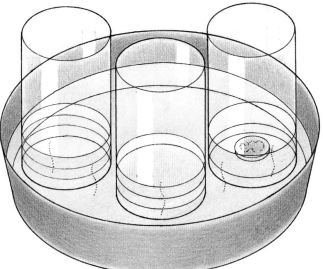

Activity 3

Have a grown-up help you fill one glass half full with hot water from the tap. Set the jar lid on the glass, upside down. Then place an ice cube on the lid. After five minutes, remove the ice cube and carefully remove the lid. What do you see on the side that covered the glass?

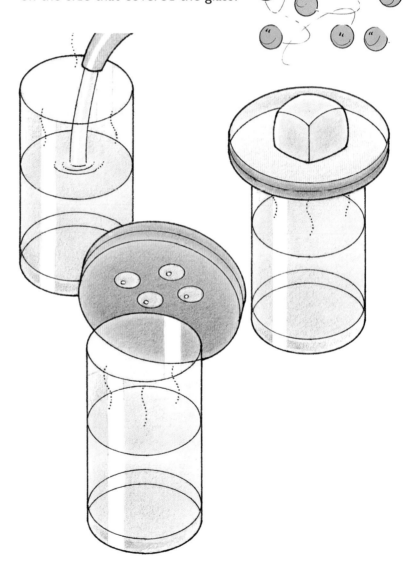

Observations

Activity 1

At room temperature, some of the ice cube melts.
The butter doesn't melt, but it gets softer. The coin
doesn't change.

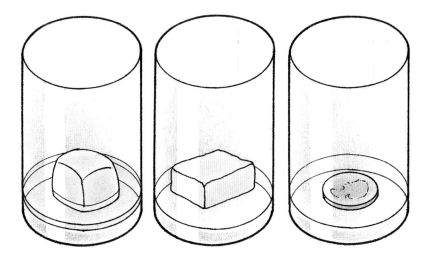

Activity 2

The hot water makes the molecules speed up. Much
more of the ice cube melts. The butter melts, too.
But the atoms in the coin don't speed up much, so it
doesn't melt.

Activity 3

There are drops of water on the lid. Some molecules
in the hot water changed to gas. But when they hit
the cold lid, they slowed down, condensed, and
became a liquid again.

The Fire Bringer

Long ago, people learned to use fire for heat and light. The Paiute Indians told this story of how a brave coyote gave them the precious gift of fire.

There was a time, long, long ago, when the Paiute people did not have fire. When winter came, with its bitter cold and long nights, the people wrapped themselves in rabbit skins and huddled in their underground pit-houses.

Among the Paiute there was one boy who thought only of the others. He was as cold as anyone, but it bothered him to see his people so unhappy. One day, as he sat shivering on a snowy hillside, Coyote came to him. "Why are you troubled, boy?" Coyote asked.

"I sorrow for my people," answered the boy. "They are suffering from the cold."

"There is something that can be done," said Coyote. "It will be very hard to do, but I will help you. We must bring fire to your people."

"Fire? What is fire?" asked the boy.

"It is like a bright, red flower, but it is not a flower," Coyote said. "Nor is it a beast, even though, like a beast, it devours grass and woods and everything in its path. But if it is kept inside a circle of stones, it will be a friend to your people. It will give them light and keep them warm."

"Where is this fire?" asked the boy.

"Its den is on the Burning Mountain by the Big Water, more than a hundred days' journey from here," Coyote told him. "It is guarded day and night by the Fire Spirits. Perhaps I can creep close enough to steal some of the fire and give it to you."

The boy leaped to his feet. "Let us go, my friend."

"Wait," warned Coyote. "It will not be easy. The Fire Spirits will chase us. You could never run for a hundred days without them catching you! You must gather a hundred of your tribe's swiftest runners, each waiting a day's distance apart."

So the boy went among his people and told them the things Coyote had said. But many did not believe him. "How can you, only a boy, know about this 'fire'?" they asked scornfully.

But the boy pleaded and argued. Finally the people decided that they had nothing to lose. They chose one hundred of the tribe's swiftest runners. Then the runners, along with the boy and Coyote, left their homeland. They journeyed into the great mountains whose peaks touched the sky.

At the end of each day, Coyote told one of the runners, "You will be the last runner. Wait here. In time, you will see a runner coming toward you, carrying a stick upon which a bright, red flower is

growing. That is the fire. You must take the fire from the runner and run home as fast as you can."

The group waded through mountain streams. They followed dark forest trails. Finally, they crossed a vast, parched plain toward the horizon that was hidden in a blue mist.

One by one, the runners were left behind. At the end of the hundredth day, Coyote and the boy stood at the foot of the great, black cone of the Burning Mountain. From its peak, there rose a plume of smoke. The Fire Spirits danced, and the flames glared red on the Big Water.

Coyote picked up a dry
branch. "When you see me
come back, be ready to run,"
he said. Then he set off up
the mountain.

The tired, dirty Coyote
crept toward the Fire Spirits.
They laughed to see this

shabby, skinny, slinking creature, so hungry he was chewing on an old tree branch. They paid no more attention to him—which was exactly what Coyote wanted. The Fire Spirits continued their dance. Suddenly, Coyote leaped forward and caught a bit of fire on the branch. The astonished Fire Spirits screamed in rage. Swift as the wind, they chased Coyote down the mountain.

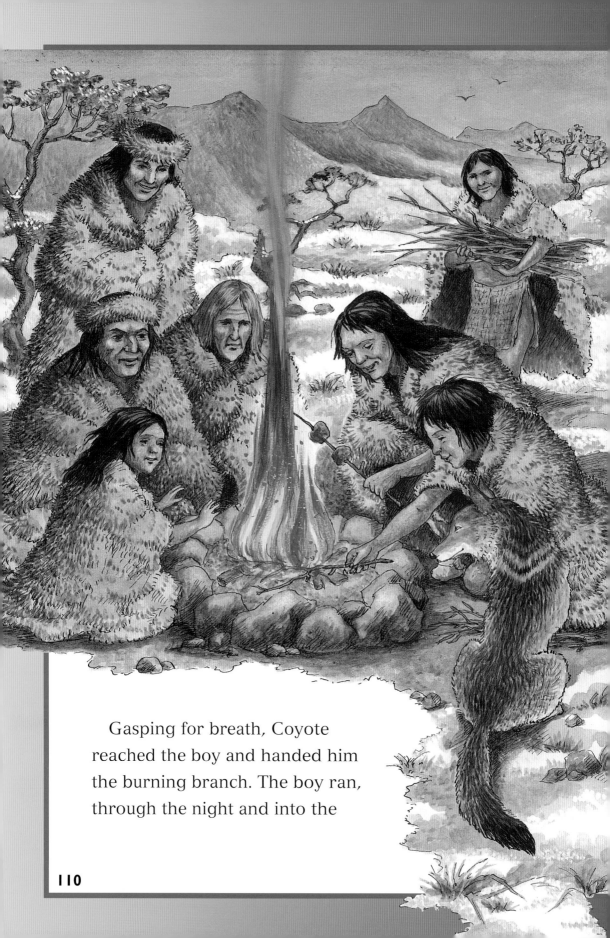

Gasping for breath, Coyote
reached the boy and handed him
the burning branch. The boy ran,
through the night and into the

next day, with the Fire Spirits hissing and crackling behind him. Dizzy with exhaustion, the boy finally handed off the flaming branch to the next runner.

And so the torch passed from one runner to the next. They sped over the parched plains and through the dark woods. Behind them, always, hissed the furious Fire Spirits. But when the Fire Sprits reached the snowy mountains, they could not go on. Fire cannot live on snow.

Finally, the last runner arrived at the Paiute lands with the burning branch. The people set up a ring of stones around the fire, as Coyote had told them. The fire blazed, and the people crowded about, marveling at the light, warmth, and comfort it gave them.

In honor of his great achievement, the people named the boy Fire Bringer. And they remembered the bravery of Coyote, too.

Since then, every coyote's fur has carried the dark scorch marks of the angry Fire Spirits who guard the Burning Mountain.

What Happens with Light?

Sleepily, you open your eyes. Sunlight is streaming through your window. It is time to get up and start your day.

The sunshine lit up your room and woke you. But the light from the sun does much more than that. It makes life on the earth possible.

Sunlight gives us energy. This energy heats the earth so that animals, plants, and people can live. It also makes green plants grow. All the food we eat comes from plants or from animals that eat plants.

Light is so important that people have invented ways to make it. We have candles, flashlights, electric lights, neon signs, and lasers. All these things help us to see. But light does other things, too. Read on and learn all about the amazing energy called light.

What Is Light?

A burning candle has a soft, glowing flame that gives off light. But when you turn on a light bulb, there is no flame. So how does a light bulb give off light?

When the light is on, **electricity** runs through a tiny wire inside the bulb. This makes the wire hot. And when the wire gets hot enough, something begins to happen.

Like everything else, the wire is made of tiny bits of matter called **atoms**. As the wire in the light bulb gets hot, the

atoms soak up **energy**. Pretty soon, the
atoms have soaked up all the energy
they can hold. Then they begin to throw
off the extra energy as light.

Anything that is hot enough gives off
light. And something as big and as hot
as the sun gives off a tremendous
amount of light. The sun's temperature
is thousands of times hotter than
anything on the earth. So the sun keeps
its atoms jumping. And the atoms
keep pouring out bundles and bundles
of light.

Bouncing Light

A full moon gives enough light for a game of hide-and-seek or for an evening walk. Where does the bright, silvery light of the moon come from? You might be surprised to learn that it comes from the sun! The moon shines only because the sun shines on it. Some of the sun's light is **reflected**, or bounced off, the moon and hits the earth. So what we call "moonlight" is actually reflected light from the sun.

TRY THIS!
1

You can see for yourself how light bounces off things. Hold a mirror so that sunlight bounces off it and hits something else.

Some of the things we see—light bulbs, neon signs, traffic lights, and even television tubes—are like the sun. They give off light. But most of the things we see are like the moon. They have no light of their own. Light from the sun, or a lamp, or something else shines on them. They reflect that light into our eyes, and the reflected light tells us the shapes, sizes, and colors of these things.

Turn out the light in your room one night. If there is no light from a lamp or a window to bounce off things, you cannot see them. Everything is dark. When the lights are turned on, reflected light shows us what is there.

The moon shines when light from the sun bounces off it. That light then bounces off the water, making the water shine.

117

What Makes a Shadow?

In the sunshine, your shadow travels everywhere with you. Sometimes it bends in funny places. And sometimes it bends into a strange shape. But as long as the sun shines, your shadow is always there. On a very cloudy day, or in a dark room, you have no shadow at all. Where does your shadow go? What is your shadow?

We have shadows because light moves in a certain way. It moves in waves, something like ripples in water. As long as nothing is in the way, the light waves move in one direction. But when the light waves hit an object, they are stopped. Then, on the other side of the object that stopped the light waves, there is a dark space—a shadow.

Objects in a dark room have no shadows because there are no light waves traveling through the room. On cloudy days, shadows are harder to see because the clouds break up the light waves from the sun. The clouds soak up

The girl and the dog block the sun's light, making shadows in the shapes of their bodies.

some of the light waves and scatter the rest of the light waves in all directions. When the light waves scatter and bounce instead of moving in one direction, no shadows are formed.

Mirror, Mirror

Who is that person in the mirror? It seems to be another you, doing exactly what you are doing. How can a mirror "copy" you?

Your reflection is a copy of you—but it does the exact opposite of what you do.

A mirror is very smooth. The front of a mirror is made of flat, polished glass. Behind the glass is a thin layer of silver or some other kind of shiny material.

As you stand in front of a mirror, light bounces off you and passes through the glass. When the light hits the shiny layer behind the glass, it bounces straight back at you. This is why you can see yourself.

Your reflection is a good copy of you. But have you ever noticed that your reflection does the exact opposite of what you do? If you hold out your right hand, your reflection holds out its left hand. Each part of you

Have you ever looked at yourself in a funhouse mirror? Did it make you laugh? You may look very short and fat or very tall and skinny. Funhouse mirrors are curved. Curved mirrors bend light differently than flat mirrors. Bent light makes the image that is reflected look different, too.

makes the opposite part of your reflection in the mirror.

What do you think will happen if you print your name and hold it up to a mirror? Try it and see.

Close-Ups

Its huge, glittering eyes stare at you. Its big mouth opens and closes, opens and closes. But suddenly it swims to the other side of the bowl. And it's only a goldfish after all.

Why did the goldfish look so big when it swam next to the curved glass? The bowl filled with water acted as a **lens**. The curved bowl bent the light that bounced off the goldfish and came through the bowl. This made the goldfish look much bigger than it really is.

Anything—even a drop of water—can be a lens if it is curved and if light can pass through it. A curved shape

Let a drop of water drip from your fingertip onto a coin. The curve of the water drop acts as a lens and makes the writing on the coin look bigger.

makes light bend and spread. And
spreading the light that bounces off
something makes that thing look bigger.
A lens with the right curve will
make something look larger or
closer than it really is.

A magnifying glass is just a
single lens with two curved sides. You
can use it for a close-up look at things like
paper, cloth, or even your finger. Move it
closer and then farther from the object
you are looking at. You will get a sharp,
clear view, and you may be amazed at
what you see!

Seeing Things That Aren't There

Can a lake vanish? A few minutes ago you saw cool water shimmering just up the road. But now all you see is miles of hot, paved highway. Where is the lake?

The disappearing lake is a mirage (muh RAHZH)—something that isn't what it seems to be. The mirage is made by light reflected from something far away. You may see a mirage when layers of cool air and warm air are close to the earth.

Light usually travels in a straight line. But when light passes through layers of warm air and cool air, it acts differently. The warm layers and cool layers act like a lens. A lens is a curved piece of glass or plastic that bends light to make things look bigger or smaller. The warm and cool layers bend the light.

If the bottom layer of air is warm, the mirage will be close to the ground. But if the bottom layer is cold, the light will bend the other way. The mirage will be high up—it may even seem to float in the air!

A mirage can come from surprising places. A "lake" may be light waves from far-off clouds. A rocky "island" may be light waves from a distant mountaintop. People at sea have seen "ghost ships" floating upside down in the sky—images of real ships far away on another part of the ocean. And people sailing on the Strait of Messina off the coast of Italy sometimes see an "enchanted city" floating in the water!

The water in this picture is real, but the sailboat and its reflection are both mirages.

Smile for the Camera

There you are with that teddy bear you had when you were 2 years old. And here you are with that big fish you caught last summer. Both times, someone took your picture. The camera made a copy of the way you looked.

A camera makes a copy of what it "sees" through its lens.

A camera has a lens that bends light rays and makes them focus, or come together, on the film inside. The light "prints" a picture on the film.

The camera has a small opening called a shutter. Most of the time, the shutter is closed. When you press a button, the shutter opens for just a small part of a second to let the light hit the film.

After you take a picture, the film rolls inside the camera. The picture you just took moves out of the way and a new piece of film moves into place. Next, you

look through a tiny window called a viewfinder to see what will be in the picture. Finally, you press the button. The shutter opens and closes. When the film is developed, you will have a picture you can keep—a picture that shows what you and the camera saw.

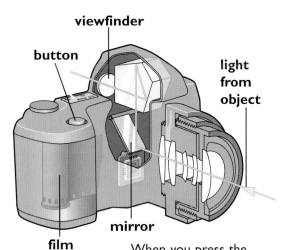

When you press the button, the camera lets the light in very quickly. It makes a picture on the film.

What you see in the camera's viewfinder is what will be in the picture.

What Is Color?

The cheese in your sandwich is orange. The tomato is bright red. The lettuce is green. The light brown bread has a dark brown crust.

We see colors in things because of the way they reflect light. But the colors are really in the light. The light from the sun is a mixture of all colors. We call this type of light **white light**.

You can see these colors if you shine bright sunlight through a special glass called a **prism** (PRIHZ uhm). When white light goes through a prism, it spreads and separates into a band of colors, like a rainbow. It has six bands of color—violet, blue, green, yellow, orange, and red.

When white light shines on something, that object **absorbs**, or soaks up, some of these colors. But it reflects other colors. Objects appear to be the colors they reflect. So the tomato in your sandwich looks red because it reflects red and absorbs other colors. Lettuce reflects green.

The paper on this page looks white because it reflects all the colors. The words look black because they reflect almost no light at all. Black objects absorb nearly all the light that reaches them. So you don't see any color in something that is black.

A prism splits light into different colors.

A World of Colors

Think of sunsets and traffic lights, campfires and television screens. They all give off light in many colors. What makes the colors different? Why do we see so many colors?

All the colors of light are given off in the same way. When atoms are heated, they soak up energy. Then they give off the energy as bundles of light.

The heat of this lava flow gives off light in beautiful colors.

All light comes from atoms. It is produced by atoms that have gained energy. For example, atoms take up energy when they are heated. Then they give up energy in the form of light.

This light may have a lot of energy, or just a little. The color of the light depends on the amount of energy it has. In the visible spectrum, red light has the least energy. After red, come orange, yellow, green, and blue. Violet light has the most energy.

In the visible spectrum, blue light has more energy than every color except violet.

Part of the energy stored in wood is given off as light when the wood is burned.

Colors We Don't See

Sun lamps make artificial ultraviolet rays. The energy given off by a sun lamp is like the ultraviolet rays found in natural light. People should use great care when using sun lamps. The strength of light they make is much more powerful than sunlight.

Ouch! You went swimming all day and forgot to put on more sunscreen after you got out of the water. Now you have a stinging sunburn. How did you get it? Your sunburn came from light, but not from light that you can see.

When all the colors in sunlight are separated, they make a rainbow. The rainbow has a band of red on one edge and a band of violet on the other edge.

In between are all the other colors. But beyond the red edge and the violet edge, there are "colors" you do not see.

A suntan or a painful sunburn both come from **ultraviolet** (UHL truh VY uh liht) rays. Ultraviolet means "beyond violet." Ultraviolet rays are just beyond the violet edge of the rainbow. You cannot see these rays. But when your skin tans or burns, you see what their energy can do.

The heat you feel when the sun is bright comes from **infrared** (IHN fruh REHD) rays. Infrared means "below red." Infrared rays are just below the red edge of the rainbow. These rays can't be seen either. But you can feel them. When they hit something, the energy they give off makes that object heat up. Sidewalks get hot in summer because they absorb energy from the sun's infrared rays.

But when photographed in ultraviolet light, *below,* dark areas appear that resemble the markings seen by bees.

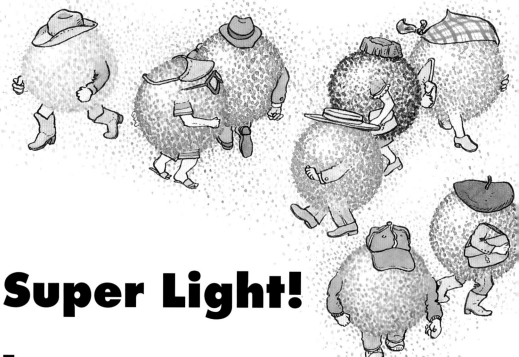

Super Light!

It punches through steel. It performs tiny, delicate operations. Is it a superhero? No, it is a special kind of light. The light that can do these things is called a **laser** (LAY zuhr) beam. A laser beam is made up of bundles of energy called **photons** (FOH tahnz), just like ordinary light. But the photons in a laser beam act in an unusual way.

The photons in ordinary light have different amounts of energy. They go in all directions, and they start and stop at different times. They are like people in a crowd, walking in all different directions. But in laser light, all the photons work in the same way. They are exactly the same color, so they all have the same amount of energy. They are also given off at regular times, and they travel in only one direction. They are like marchers in a parade.

With all the photons moving together, laser light is very powerful. But don't worry! You aren't going to run into any laser beams out on the street. Laser beams have to be made in special machines. Then they can burn through metal or even drill a tiny hole in a diamond.

Light Through Wires

You can talk on the phone to someone who is far away. You can press a button and see a television show from another country. These sounds and pictures may be traveling to you in the form of light.

Fiber-optic (FY buhr AHP tihk) **cables** make this possible. These cables are made from clear glass or plastic strands—sometimes as thin as a hair. These strands or fibers are gathered into bundles and wrapped in a special covering. Light travels very fast through

Hello! How are you?

each one of these strands. And the light
can carry messages faster and more
clearly than old-fashioned copper wires.

Here is how a phone call in a fiber-optic
system works. When you talk to a friend,
the phone changes the sound of your
voice into electric signals. Then a laser at
one end of the fiber changes these
electric signals into high-speed flashes of
light. At the other end of the fiber, a
special device changes the flashes back
into electric signals. Your friend's phone
then changes these signals back into the
sound of your voice.

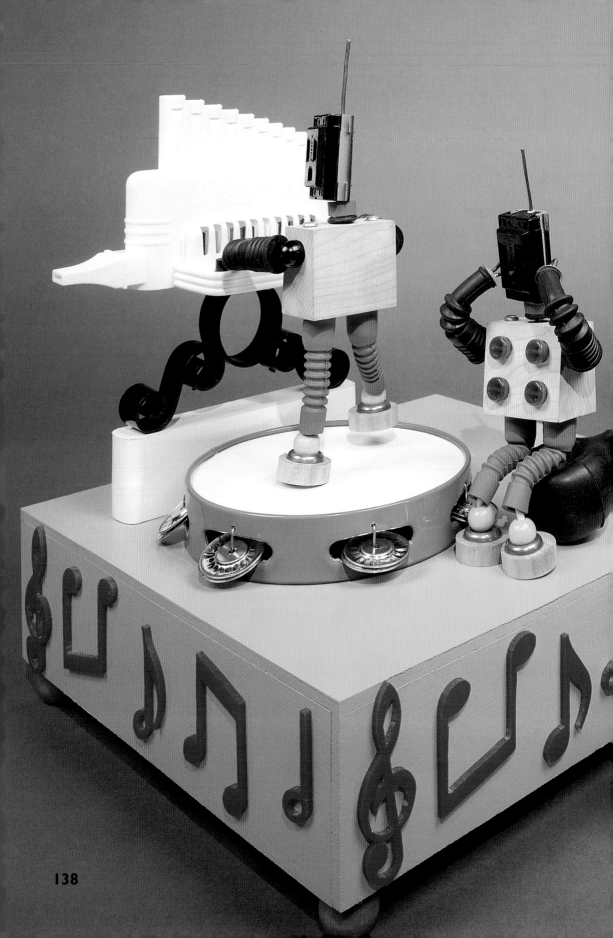

What Happens with Sound?

Sound comes from just about everywhere—from friends talking, radios playing, and jet planes roaring overhead. Even your breathing makes a tiny sound.

All the sounds you hear—high and low sounds, loud and soft sounds, bouncing and traveling sounds— are alike in one way: they are made when something moves.

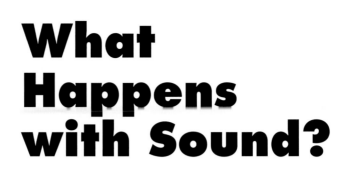

What Is Sound?

Sounds are made when something moves back and forth quickly. The back-and-forth movements that make sound are called **vibrations** (vy BRAY shuhnz). Usually, the movements are too tiny for you to see. The vibrations travel through the air, almost the same way that waves travel across water. When the vibrations reach our ears, we hear them as sounds.

Vibrations are **energy**—sound energy. Sound is made up of tiny pushes and pulls. When the vibrations stop, the sound stops, too. You don't hear another sound until things start vibrating again.

See for yourself how sound waves travel through the air.

Stretch plastic wrap tightly over the open end of a glass. Use a rubber band to keep the plastic in place. Sprinkle a few rice grains over the plastic. Hold a baking pan close to the glass and bang it with a wooden spoon. What happens? The traveling sound waves hit the plastic wrap and made it vibrate. The vibration makes the rice grains bounce.

Now You Hear It, Now You Don't

A ticking clock sounds loud when you put your ear close to it. As you walk away, the ticking gets softer and softer, until you can't hear the ticking at all. Why does the sound get softer?

The ticking you hear is made by the moving parts of the clock. The movement of these parts—the tiny pushes and pulls—makes the air around the clock move. It pushes the air **molecules** together into sound waves.

The sound waves from the clock spread out in all directions. They move through the air to your ear, and you hear the ticking.

The sound waves are strongest at the point where they are made—close to the vibrating clock. So when you stand next to the clock, the ticking is loud. But as the sound waves spread out through the air, they grow weaker and weaker. So as you move away from the clock, the ticking gets softer.

By the time the sound waves have traveled across the room, the air is hardly moving at all. The pushes and pulls are too tiny for your ears to pick up, so you no longer hear the sound of the ticking clock.

Sound Gets Around

A swimming fish seems to glide through the water without making a sound. But it doesn't swim as quietly as you think. Divers swimming underwater hear a loud crack when a large fish flips its tail and darts away.

Most of the everyday sounds we hear travel through air. But sound waves travel through liquids and solids, too. Things like water, wood, and even the earth can **conduct**, or carry, these vibrations. You know this is true if you've ever heard noise coming from a closed room. Sound travels through walls and doors.

The molecules of liquids and solids are closer together than the molecules in air. And in some liquids and solids, the molecules are "springy." They bounce back like a rubber band when they are pushed.

These kinds of molecules vibrate easily when a sound wave pushes them. And they make nearby molecules vibrate, too. So in a solid or liquid with "springy" molecules, sound travels even faster than it travels through air.

TRY THIS! 1

Can sound travel through other things besides air? You and a friend can find out. Put your ear to a wooden tabletop. Have your friend knock or tap on the table. What do you hear? Now plug your other ear with your finger. Is the sound different?

A loud sound takes about 5 seconds to reach you if it travels 1 mile (1.6 kilometers) through air. But underwater, the same sound reaches you in little more than a second. And a sound wave zips through 1 mile (1.6 kilometers) of steel wire in about 1/3 second. This is almost 15 times faster than it travels through air.

Make a Tin-Can Telephone

This telephone doesn't need electricity to work. A piece of thread carries the sound of your voice.

You Will Need:

a hammer
2 tin cans
3 nails, 1 large and
  2 small
12 feet (3.6 meters)
  of strong thread

What To Do:

1. Have a grown-up use the hammer and the large nail to punch a hole in the center of the bottom of each can. Push the ends of the thread through the holes, from the outside to the inside of each can.

2. Tie each end of the thread to a small nail. Pull the thread until the nail touches the bottom of the can. Your "telephone" is now ready to use.

3. Give a friend one of the cans. Stand far enough apart to stretch the thread tightly. Talk softly into your end of the "telephone," while your friend holds the other can to one ear. Then have your friend talk while you listen.

When you talk, your voice makes the bottom of the can vibrate. The vibrations travel through the tight thread and the nail. When the vibrations reach the other end of the thread, they make the bottom of the second can vibrate—and your friend hears what you say.

In a real phone, electricity turns sound energy— your voice—into electrical signals. The phone on the other end turns the electrical signals back into the sound of your voice.

High and Low

Zzzeee goes the tiny mosquito as it zips past your ear. VROOOM growls a big tractor as it rumbles past you. The sound the mosquito makes is much higher than the sound of the tractor. Why are the sounds different?

When something vibrates, sound travels outward from it in waves. Each vibration—each complete back-and-forth motion—makes a single sound wave. The faster something vibrates, the more sound waves it makes and the higher the pitch.

A mosquito makes high-pitched sounds because its wings vibrate very fast— about a thousand times a second!

When you ring a small bell, it vibrates quickly, making a high ringing sound.

When you ring a large bell, it vibrates more slowly, making a lower ringing sound.

A tractor makes low-pitched sounds because its heavy metal parts vibrate slowly. The slow vibrations make only a few sound waves every second—the low rumble that you hear.

Sound from Moving Things

Have you ever noticed a change in the "whistle" a train makes as it rushes by? If you listen to a passing train, you'll notice that the sound gets higher and then lower as the train goes past you.

Actually, the whistle makes the same sound all the time. The sound seems to change because the train is passing you.

The sound spreads out in all directions from the train. But because the train is moving, each

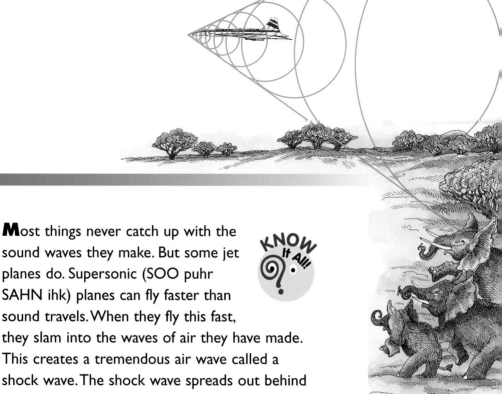

Most things never catch up with the sound waves they make. But some jet planes do. Supersonic (SOO puhr SAHN ihk) planes can fly faster than sound travels. When they fly this fast, they slam into the waves of air they have made. This creates a tremendous air wave called a shock wave. The shock wave spreads out behind the plane in a funnel shape. Traveling at the speed of sound, it crashes into the air and the ground. This makes a huge exploding noise called a **sonic** (SAHN ihk) **boom**.

KNOW It All!

sound wave starts a little ahead of the place where the last one started. This makes the sound waves ahead of the train bunch up so that more of the waves reach your ear every second. And the more waves that reach your ear in a second, the higher the sound.

But behind the train, the waves are spread apart. As the train speeds away, fewer waves reach your ear each second—so the sound gets lower.

Hello...

Hello...

What happens when you shout a big "hello" near a mountain, or between tall buildings, or in a large, empty hall? Well, you may hear an echo, another "hello" just like the one you said.

Sound bounces off hard, smooth things the way a ball bounces off a wall. The echo of your "hello" is **reflected** sound— sound that bounces back to you.

Why don't you always hear echoes? It depends on how far the sound goes before it bounces. In a small room, the sound you make travels only a short distance before it bounces. It comes back so fast that it seems like part of what you are saying.

Hello . . .

But in a very large room, the sound travels a while before it bounces back. By the time the sound comes back, you have finished speaking. So you hear the sound a second time.

You can hear the sound you make again, and again, and again! For example, if you shout between two tall buildings, the sound bounces back and forth between the walls. When that happens, the sound is reflected back to you from more than one spot. You hear "hello . . . hello . . . hello . . . " from each reflected sound. As the reflections get weaker and weaker, the sound dies out and the echoes finally stop.

Making Sound Bounce

Sound waves bounce off hard surfaces such as walls and floors and ceilings. Here is a way you can prove this by making sound waves bounce around a corner.

You Will Need:

2 cardboard tubes of
    the same size
transparent tape
a towel
a clock, watch, or timer
    that ticks
a piece of cardboard

What To Do:

1. Fasten the tubes together with the tape so that they form a corner.

2. Place a folded towel at the free end of one of the tubes. Place the watch on the towel.

3. Put your ear close to the free end of the second tube. Can you hear the watch ticking? No? Try it another way.

4. Lean the piece of cardboard across the open space between the tubes. Now put your ear close to the second tube. What happens this time? Now you can hear the ticking. Do you know why?

The sound waves made by the ticking watch travel though the first tube. But when the space between the tubes is open, the sound waves simply go out the open end. There is no way for them to get into the second tube.

When you place the cardboard across the open space, the sound waves bounce off the cardboard and into the second tube. The second tube carries the sound to your ear, and you hear the watch ticking. And that's how you can make sound go around a corner.

Measuring Sound

Vibrating strings give this Egyptian instrument its special sound.

Sounds can be high or low. But they can also be loud or soft. What makes a sound loud or soft?

Sounds are the vibrations, or back-and-forth movements, made by moving objects. Strong vibrations make strong sounds. Vibrations are strong when an object moves a lot.

A string on an instrument like a guitar is silent when it is still, *top*. But when a player plucks it, it vibrates and makes sound, *bottom*.

You can make a sound by stretching a thick rubber band and then plucking it with your fingers. If you pluck the rubber band hard, the back-and-forth movements are bigger. Bigger movements make a louder sound. If you pluck the rubber band lightly, the back-and-forth movements are smaller. So the sound is softer.

Scientists measure the strength of a sound in units called decibels (DEHS uh buhlz). A sound of zero decibels is the weakest sound a person with normal hearing can hear. A sound of 140 decibels hurts your ears.

KNOW It All!

The basic unit scientists use to measure sound is the bel. The bel was named after Alexander Graham Bell, the inventor of the telephone. We usually measure sounds in units called decibels. *Deci* means "one-tenth." So a decibel is one-tenth of a bel.

Shhhh!

Rattling trucks, roaring jets, squeaking chalk, and creaking doors don't make music. They make sounds that disturb us—sounds we don't want to hear. These unwanted sounds are called noise.

Noise is hard to stop. Like other sounds, noise travels through air and through solid things—even through walls.

But some materials actually soak up noise. They absorb sound waves and keep them from traveling. Inside a building, rugs and curtains soak up sound. The soft threads and tiny air spaces in the material help trap the vibrations. Special ceiling tile can trap sound vibrations, too. The tile is full of tiny holes, like a sponge. When sound waves strike the tile, they bounce around inside the holes until they get weaker and die away.

People who work with airplanes and other heavy machines wear special helmets and earmuffs to cover their ears while they are working. The sound-absorbing material shuts out most of the noise that could bother them or even hurt their ears.

KNOW It **All!**

There is a special branch of science that deals with the way sound affects people. This science is known as acoustics (uh KOOS tihks). Acoustics helps people design theaters so that music sounds good. It also helps them figure out how to control harmful noise. Scientists even use acoustics to study how we make and understand sounds.

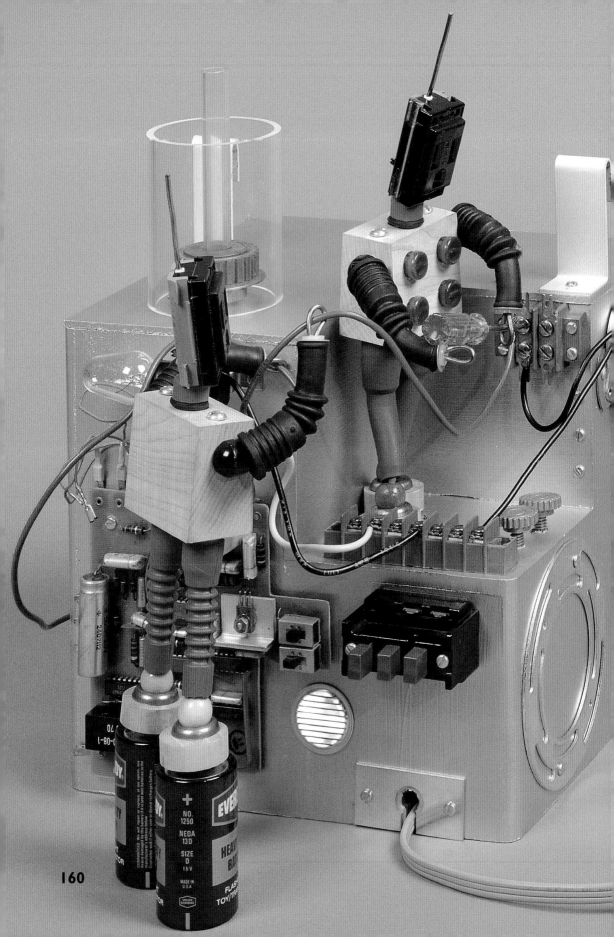

What Happens with Electricity?

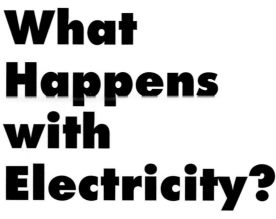

When you turn on a light, ring a doorbell, or plug in a toaster, you start a parade. But it's a parade you can't see! It's a parade of moving bits of energy that are called electrons (ih LEHK trahnz). Inside every electric wire, there are millions of electrons. When you press a button or turn a switch, they move through the wire. They make a strong push that gets work done. The energy of the moving electrons is called electricity. It makes the light, the doorbell, and the toaster work.

Making Sparks Fly

Have you ever felt sparks fly when you pulled your jacket off? Or did you ever get a crackling shock when you touched a doorknob? These things happen because your body has been collecting **electricity**.

The sparks and crackles are called **static** (STAT ihk) **electricity**—electrons that pile up in one place. On cool, dry days, you scrape **electrons** loose from things. When you walk across a rug, or when your jacket rubs against you, the loose electrons stick to your body.

The loose electrons cannot flow through you. But they can jump from you to a material that has fewer electrons. So when you touch a doorknob or pull off your jacket, that's exactly what happens. Then you hear the crackle of jumping electrons—and sometimes you feel it, too!

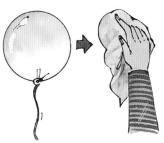

See the pull that electrons make by creating your own sticky balloon. Blow up a balloon and tie a piece of string to it. Rub the balloon with a wool cloth. Then touch the balloon to the cloth and let go of the string. When you rub the balloon with the cloth, it picks up electrons from the cloth.

The balloon then has more electrons than the cloth. When you put the balloon next to the cloth, the piled-up electrons on the balloon begin to move back to the cloth. They pull so hard that the balloon sticks to the cloth. That's static electricity!

TRY THIS!
1

A Push in a Wire

Click! When you turn on a lamp, a light bulb glows. When you turn on a radio, sounds come out. But electricity doesn't just jump into the lamp or the radio. It flows through wires.

The lamp and the radio run on an electric **current** (KUHR uhnt). An electric current travels along a pathway made of wires.

The center of the wire is made of metal, such as copper. Metals have electrons that are free to move. So the electrons can move along the metal. The outside of the wire is made of rubber or plastic. The electrons in rubber or plastic are held tightly to their **atoms.** They can't move from one atom to another.

When the electric current is turned on, the metal part of the wire **conducts** (kuhn DUHKTS), or carries, the electricity. The electrons push along the wire from atom to atom, conducting electrical energy. But the plastic or rubber covering doesn't conduct electricity. So, the rubber or plastic covering **insulates** (IN suh layts), or seals off, the wire. It keeps the moving electrons from leaving the path to your lamp or radio.

The inside of a wire is made of a metal. The outside is made of rubber or plastic.

It's Light!

When you turn on a lamp, electricity makes the bulb light up. How?

The electricity flows through a wire into the bulb. It travels around a wire inside the bulb. Then it leaves the bulb. Part of the path through the bulb is a filament (FIHL uh muht), a very thin thread of coiled wire. The filament is so thin that electrons have to push hard to get through.

Electricity traveling through the thin wire of a light bulb makes the bulb glow.

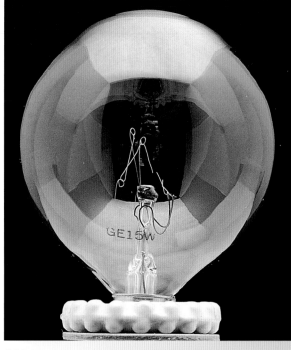

When the wire in the bulb breaks, the electricity stops flowing. The bulb is burned out.

The push of the electrons makes the molecules in the filament move faster. As the molecules speed up, they get so hot that their electrons give off energy. Then the filament glows.

The filament in the light bulb is made of a metal called tungsten (TUHNG stuhn). A tungsten wire can get very hot without burning or melting. But as tungsten is heated, its molecules very slowly change to a gas and leave the wire. So, as the light bulb glows, the filament gets thinner and thinner.

After many hours of use, the filament breaks. The bulb is "burnt out." The electricity can't get across the break in the filament. Then you put in a new bulb. Now the electric current has a path to follow. The lamp lights up again.

The famous American inventor Thomas Edison created the first light bulb in 1879.

When you use electricity to iron your clothes or toast your bread, two things happen. Electricity makes a strong push in a wire, and the wire pushes back!

Electricity makes the iron and the toaster heat up. The electricity travels into and out of these machines on wire pathways. Most of the pathways conduct electricity easily, so the electrons are free to move.

But inside the iron and the toaster, part of the pathway is made of a different kind of wire. This wire is made from a kind of metal in which the electrons don't move very easily. Often the wire is very thin, and sometimes it is wound into a long, tight coil. Instead of conducting electricity easily, this part of the pathway **resists** (rih ZIHSTS) the current. The electrons have to push hard to move through this wire.

The pushing electrons make the molecules in the wire speed up and bump one another. The harder they bump and push, the hotter the wire gets. In a few minutes, the bumping and pushing make the wire hot. And the heat presses clothes or toasts bread.

Charge!

An electric current is a push in a wire—the push of moving electrons. But what makes the electrons start to push through the wire? Where does the current come from?

The current is made in a kind of "electricity factory" called a power plant. The special machine that makes electricity is called a **generator** (JEHN uh RAY tuhr).

A generator uses a huge, spinning magnet to make electrons move. The pull of the spinning magnet is strong enough to start electrons pushing in a wire.

The magnet is surrounded by a large coil of tightly wound wire. When the magnet begins to spin, its pull starts millions of electrons pushing! This push makes a strong electric current in the coiled wire. The current is sent through other wires from the power plant to your home.

A generator makes electrical energy. But a generator uses energy, too. Running water, burning fuel, or nuclear

energy runs the engines or other
machines that make the huge magnets
spin. So a generator actually is an
energy-changing machine. It changes
other kinds of energy into electrical
energy—energy you can use.

Starting and Stopping the Push

You want your electric clock to run day and night. But you wouldn't want your doorbell ringing all the time. Things like doorbells, lamps, and radios work only when you turn them on.

Most things that run by electricity have a switch. A switch is used to turn the electric current on and off. The electric current moves along the wirc and across the switch to another wire inside the bell, lamp, or radio. The switch is a "bridge" in the path the electricity follows.

A metal piece inside the switch moves when you turn the switch on and off. When you turn the switch on, the metal piece touches both wires. The "bridge" is down. The electricity coming into the switch can cross the "bridge" and keep traveling along the pathway.

When you turn the switch off, the metal piece moves away from the wire. The "bridge" is up. Without the "bridge," the electric current can't cross the switch and follow the path. So, the electric current stops moving, and things stop working until you lower the "bridge" in the pathway by turning the switch on again.

Packages of Electricity

A flashlight runs on electricity, but you don't have to plug it in. It carries its own electric current in a "package"—a battery.

A battery is made of layers of chemicals inside a metal container. When the flashlight is turned on, some of the chemicals in the battery break apart and eat away at the metal container. As this happens, some of the metal atoms leave the container and combine with the chemicals inside the battery.

Parts of a battery

metal container

paper or
plastic jacket

layers of
chemicals

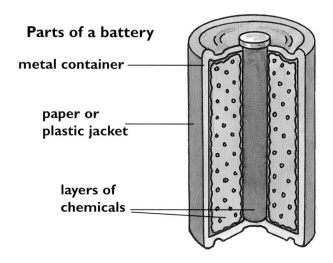

As the metal atoms move away from the container, they leave some of their electrons behind. So the container gains electrons. And as the chemicals inside the battery break apart, they lose electrons.

Soon, there are more electrons in the container than there are inside the battery. Then the extra electrons in the container begin to move out of the battery. They travel through the bulb and back into the middle of the battery, where electrons are scarce. The push of these electrons is the current that makes your flashlight shine.

It may sound as if everything happens very slowly, but, as you know, it all takes place in an instant.

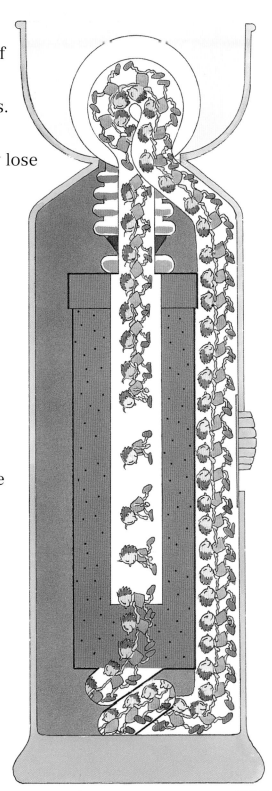

Electrons traveling from the battery to the bulb light a flashlight.

An On-Off Magnet

A powerful electromagnet can pick up pieces of steel and other metals.

Electricity can make light and heat. It can also make a magnet. But this is a magnet you can turn on and off.

A magnet made with electricity is called an **electromagnet** (ih LEHK troh MAG niht). An electromagnet has two parts. The first part is a solid center, or core, made of iron. The second part is an outer covering made of wire that is coiled around and around the core.

When an electric current runs through the wound wire, the iron becomes a magnet. The iron gets its pull, or magnetism, from the moving electrons in the wire. As soon as the electric current is turned off, an electromagnet loses its magnetism.

Electromagnets are used to make electric motors run. A motor has two sets of these magnets—an outer set that stays in place and an inner set that moves. The inner set of electromagnets is attached to an axle—a rod that can spin. When the motor is turned on, the two sets of electromagnets push and pull against each other. That push makes the inner magnets move and spin the axle. And the spinning axle gives a push that makes the motor run.

Electrical Signals

Electricity in a wire creates the pushes and pulls that get work done. It lights lamps and runs machines. But electricity has another important use. It can carry information. Thanks to electricity's ability to carry information, we have tiny radios, handheld calculators and video games, and personal computers.

A circuit board, *below*, is made up of many circuits. Each circuit does a special job.

The use of electricity to carry electric signals is called **electronics** (ih lehk TRAHN ihks). These electric signals may

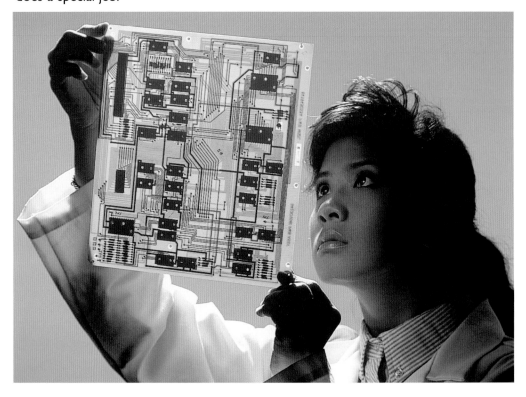

stand for sounds, pictures, numbers, letters, computer instructions, or other information.

An electronic device has many tiny electrical pathways called **circuits**. Each circuit has a special job. Some circuits store signals. Others change signals. For example, in a calculator, one circuit might add two numbers together. When the answer is reached, another circuit sends a signal that lights up a display screen to show the answer.

The circuits on most of today's electronic devices are mounted on a chip, a piece of material that is no bigger than a fingernail.

control deck

inside of controller

Inside the controller of a video game are tiny electrical circuits. When a player presses the buttons, the circuits send messages to the control deck and the video screen.

controller

Science at Work

Right now, as you are reading this book, scientists throughout the world are hard at work. Some are studying atoms and molecules. Others are making discoveries about chemicals, liquids, heat, light, motion, or sound. In fact, everything you have learned about in this book has been studied by scientists.

The sciences that you have read about in this book are called physical sciences. Physical scientists learn about how things work in the world and in outer space. They study all matter that is not alive, from tiny atoms to stars and planets.

Chemists. One of the physical sciences is chemistry. Chemists study chemicals and other materials to find out what they are made of. They also learn how these things change when they join with other substances. Chemists take molecules apart and put them together in new ways. They try to find out how chemicals can be used to make things people need, such as fuels, medicines, plastics, and thousands of other materials. Some chemists study how light, heat, and other forms of energy change chemical substances.

Chemists study chemicals and other materials to find out what they are made of and what they can do.

Physicists. Physics (FIHZ ihks) is another physical science. Scientists who study physics are called physicists (FIHZ uh sihsts). Physicists study matter, or the "stuff" all things are made of, and energy. They also study forms of energy, such as heat, light, sound, and electricity. Atomic physicists study atoms and the parts of atoms. The things learned by atomic physicists led to the invention of new weapons as well as new ways of creating energy.

These physicists are measuring the pull of gravity from high atop a television tower.

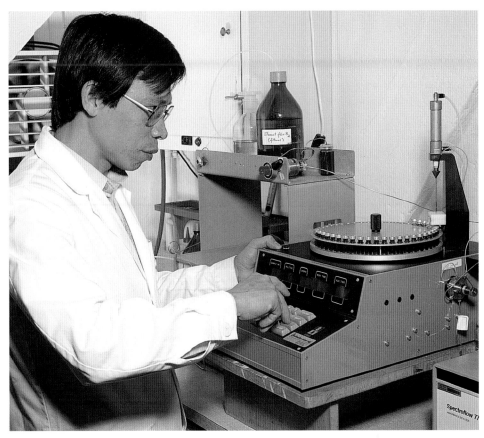

This research scientist performs tests on food in a laboratory.

Research scientists. Chemists, physicists, and all scientists who work to make new discoveries are called research scientists. They go to school for a long time to learn their subject. When they are finished with school, many research scientists work for businesses. Some work for the government of their country. Some work in universities. Do you like to find out how things work? Would you like to make guesses to explain something and then do experiments, or tests, to find out if you are right? Do you like to tell other people about your ideas and discoveries? If so, you may want to become a research scientist yourself!

Glossary

Here are some of the words you read in this book. Many of them may be new to you. Some are hard to pronounce. But since you will see them again, they are good words to know. Next to each word, you will see how to say it correctly: **electromagnet** (ih LEHK troh MAG niht). The part shown in small capital letters is said a little more loudly than the rest of the word. The part in large capital letters is said the loudest. Under each word are one or two sentences that tell what the word means.

A

absorb (ab SAWRB)
To absorb means to soak up.

atom (AT uhm)
An atom is one of the tiny particles, or bits, that all matter is made of. Most materials are made up of many kinds of atoms. But chemical elements are made up of only one type of atom.

axle (AK suhl)
An axle is the shaft around which a wheel turns.

C

chemical energy (KEHM uh kuhl EHN uhr jee)
Chemical energy is the energy stored in a fuel.

circuit (SUR kiht)
A circuit is a pathway that electrical signals travel along.

compound (KAHM pownd)
A compound is matter made of two or more different kinds of atoms joined together.

condense (kuhn DEHNS)
To condense is to turn a gas into a liquid.

conduct (kuhn DUHKT)
To conduct is to carry electricity.

current (KUR uhnt)
A current is electricity that flows through a wire.

E

electricity (ih lehk TRIHS uh tee)
Electricity is one kind of energy.

electromagnet (ih LEHK troh MAG niht)
An electromagnet is a magnet made with electricity.

electronics (ih lehk TRAHN ihks)
Electronics is the use of electricity to carry electric signals.

electrons (ih LEHK trahnz)
Electrons are tiny parts of an atom that whirl around the atom's center, or nucleus.

element (EHL uh muhnt)

An element is a kind of matter that is made up of only one kind of atom.

energy (EHN uhr jee)

A force that has the power to make things move or work is energy.

equilibrium (EE kwuh LIHB ree uhm)

An object in equilibrium is balanced. It won't move or tip over unless something pushes on it.

evaporate (ih VAP uh rayt)

To evaporate is to become a gas.

F

fiber-optic cables (FY buhr AHP tihk KAY buhlz)

Fiber-optic cables are thin glass or plastic strands gathered into bundles and wrapped in a special covering. They carry electrical signals in the form of light.

friction (FRIHK shuhn)

Friction is the rubbing of one object or kind of matter against another. Friction makes things move more and more slowly, until they stop.

fuel (FYOO uhl)

Fuel is a material that burns to create heat, light, or a push to move something.

fulcrum (FUHL kruhm)

The fulcrum is the resting place on a lever. It is often between the load and the force.

G

gas (gas)

A gas is a substance that expands to fill any container it is in. The air we breathe is made up of several kinds of gases.

gear (geer)

A gear is a wheel with teeth that makes other wheels move.

generator (JEHN uh RAY tuhr)

A generator is an electricity-making machine.

gravity (GRAV uh tee)

Gravity is a force that pulls all objects downward, toward the center of the earth.

I

inclined plane (ihn KLYND playn)

An inclined plane is a flat surface that slants.

inertia (ihn UHR shuh)

Inertia is the name for the way things that are stopped stay stopped, and things that are moving keep moving.

infrared (IHN fruh REHD)

Infrared is a raylike light. It cannot be seen, but it heats things up.

insulate (IHN suh layt)

To insulate is to hold in heat, sound, or electricity with some kind of material.

L

laser (LAY zuhr)

A laser is a machine that makes a special kind of powerful light.

lens (lenz)

A lens is a curved piece of glass or plastic that bends light and makes things look bigger or smaller.

lever (LEHV uhr)

A lever is a kind of machine that is used to move a load. It makes pushing and lifting easy, even when things are big and heavy.

liquid (LIHK wihd)

A liquid is a form of matter that can flow in all directions. It takes the shape of the container it is in.

M

molecule (MAHL uh kyool)

A molecule is a group of joined atoms. A molecule is the smallest piece a compound can be broken into and still stay the same.

N

nuclear energy (NOO klee uhr EHN uhr jee)

Nuclear energy is the energy that is released when certain kinds of atoms are split.

P

perpetual motion (puhr PEHCH oo uhl MOH shuhn)

Perpetual motion is motion that goes on forever.

photons (FOH tahnz)

Photons are tiny bundles of light energy.

physics (FIHZ ihks)

Physics is the science of how nonliving things in nature work and move in the world.

prism (PRIHZ uhm)

A prism is a piece of glass that spreads and separates white light into a band of colors—violet, blue, green, yellow, orange, and red—like a rainbow.

pulley (PUL ee)

A pulley is a special kind of wheel and axle with a rope that runs over it. A pulley is used to lift or pull things.

R

reflect (rih FLEHKT)

To reflect is to send back light from a surface.

resist (rih ZIHST)
To resist is to hold out against a force.

S
solar energy (SOH luhr EHN uhr jee)
Solar energy is energy from the sun.

solid (SAHL ihd)
A solid is a form of matter that has a shape of its own.

sonic boom (SAHN ihk boom)
A sonic boom is a huge exploding noise caused by something traveling faster than the speed of sound.

static electricity (STAT ihk ih lehk TRIHS uh tee)
Static electricity is an electric charge that builds up when electrons pile up in one place.

steam (steem)
Steam is water in the form of a hot gas.

U
ultraviolet (UHL truh VY uh liht)
Ultraviolet light is the invisible light that causes sunburn.

V
vibrations (vy BRAY shuhnz)
Vibrations are rapid back-and-forth movements.

W
wedge (wehj)
A wedge is a machine with a thin, sharp edge that can cut or push into things easily.

white light (hwyt lyt)
White light is light that contains a mixture of all colors.

Index

This index is an alphabetical list of important topics covered in this book. It will help you find information given in both words and pictures. To help you understand what an entry means, there is sometimes a helping word in parentheses, for example, **Archimedes** (scientist). If there is information in both words and pictures, you will see the words *with pictures* in parentheses after the page number. If there is only a picture, you will see the word *picture* in parentheses after the page number.

Illustration Acknowledgments

The Publishers of *Childcraft* gratefully acknowledge the courtesy of the following illustrators, photographers, agencies, and organizations for illustrations in this volume. When all the illustrations for a sequence of pages are from a single source, the inclusive page numbers are given. Credits should be read from top to bottom, left to right, on their respective pages. All illustrations are the exclusive property of the publishers of *Childcraft* unless names are marked with an asterisk(*).

Cover	Rainbow—© Ken Graham, Tony Stone Images*; Atom—Leonard C. Morgan; Kids with magnets—© Kristy McClaren*; Mir Satellite—NASA*
Back Cover	© Kristy McClaren*
1	© Kristy McClaren*; Leonard C. Morgan; NASA*
2-3	Tony Herbert; Malcolm Livingstone; Joe Rogers
4-5	Joe Rogers
6-7	Joanna Stubbs, Pat Tourret; Robert Byrd; Joe Rogers
8-9	Stan Smetkowski, CHILDCRAFT photo
10-11	Jack Wallen; CHILDCRAFT photo; Rick Incrocci
12-13	Joe Rogers
14-15	Stella Ormai; CHILDCRAFT illustration
16-17	Malcolm Livingstone; CHILDCRAFT photo; Dennis Bishop
18-19	Stella Ormai; CHILDCRAFT photo; CHILDCRAFT illustration
20-21	Joe Rogers; CHILDCRAFT photo; Joe Rogers
22-23	CHILDCRAFT illustration; Stella Ormai
24-25	Malcolm Livingstone
26-27	Rick Incrocci
28-29	Stan Smetkowski, CHILDCRAFT photo
30-31	Robert Byrd; Rick Incrocci
32-33	CHILDCRAFT photo; Jack Wallen; Tony Herbert
34-35	Jack Wallen; Joanna Stubbs and Pat Tourret; Joanna Stubbs and Pat Tourret
36-37	Robert Byrd
38-39	© Kristy McClaren*; CHILDCRAFT illustration; CHILDCRAFT illustration; Joe Rogers
40-41	David Mostyn; Eileen Mueller Neill
42-43	Robert Byrd; CHILDCRAFT illustration; © Northrop Grumman Corp.*; CHILDCRAFT illustration
44-45	Frank James; Jeremy Gower; NASA*
46-47	Gerald Witcomb; NASA*; Joe Rogers
48-49	Stan Smetkoski, CHILDCRAFT photo
50-51	The Field Museum of Natural History, Chicago (WORLD BOOK photo); Joe Rogers; Pamela Goodchild; Leonard E. Morgan
52-53	Robert Byrd; CHILDCRAFT photos;
54-55	Stella Ormai; Rick Incrocci
56-57	Tony Herbert; Friso Henstra
58-59	Stella Ormai
60-63	Eileen Mueller Neill
64-65	Stan Smetkowski, CHILDCRAFT photo
66-67	David Mostyn; Eileen Mueller Neill; David Weisner; David Mostyn
68-69	John Sandford; © David R. Frazier*
70-71	NASA*; Tom Stimpson
72-73	© W. H. Muller, Zefa Picture Library*; CHILDCRAFT photo by Gilbert Meyers; Malcolm Livingstone
74-75	Malcolm Livingstone
76-77	David Weisner
78-79	Eileen Mueller Neill
80-81	© Thiele, Zefa Picture Library*; © H. R. Bramaz, Peter Arnold, Inc.*
82-83	CHILDCRAFT photo by Daniel D. Miller; Eileen Mueller Neill; David Weisner; Malcolm Livingstone; David Mostyn; © W. H. Muller, Zefa Picture Library*; Frank James
84-85	Kathy Clo; Rick Incrocci; Kathy Clo
86-87	Stan Smetkowski, CHILDCRAFT photo
88-89	CHILDCRAFT photo by Daniel D. Miller; Malcolm Livingstone; Malcolm Livingstone; Malcolm Livingstone; Eileen Mueller Neill
90-91	CHILDCRAFT photo; Malcolm Livingstone
92-93	CHILDCRAFT photo; Michael Chalton; CHILDCRAFT photo
94-95	Brian Cody; Grahame Corbett; Joe Rogers
96-97	Brian Cody; Rick Incrocci
98-99	Joe Rogers
100-101	Malcolm Livingstone; Grahame Corbett; Malcolm Livingstone; Grahame Corbett
102-103	Grahame Corbett; Malcolm Livingstone; Grahame Corbett
104-111	Kinuko Craft
112-113	Stan Smetkowski, CHILDCRAFT photo
114-115	Claire Smith
116-117	Oxford Illustrators Ltd.; © P. J. Sharpe, Zefa Picture Library*
118-119	Julie Durrell
120-121	CHILDCRAFT photo by Daniel D. Miller; CHILDCRAFT photo by Daniel D. Miller; © Jeremy Horner, Tony Stone Images*
122-123	Joe Rogers; Kathy Clo; Grahame Corbett
124-125	© Alistair B. Fraser*
126-127	Precision Graphics; © Sally & Richard Greenhill*; Precision Graphics
128-129	© Zefa Picture Library*
130-131	© Superstock*; © W. H. Muller, Zefa Picture Library*; © David R. Frazier*
132-133	David Weisner; © Thomas Eisner*; © Thomas Eisner*
134-135	David Weisner
136-137	Eileen Mueller Neill
138-139	Stan Smetkowski, CHILDCRAFT photo
140-141	John Sandford; Joe Rogers
142-143	Stella Ormai
144-145	Stella Ormai; John Sandford
146-147	John Sandford
148-149	Eileen Mueller Neill; Robert Byrd
150-151	Robert Byrd
152-153	Stella Ormai
154-155	CHILDCRAFT photo
156-157	© Sylvain Grandadam, Tony Stone Images*; Joe Rogers
158-159	David Mostyn
160-161	Stan Smetkowski, CHILDCRAFT photo
162-163	Nan Brooks; Rowan-Barnes-Murphy
164-165	CHILDCRAFT illustration; CHILDCRAFT photo
166-167	CHILDCRAFT photo; CHILDCRAFT photo; Friso Henstra
168-169	Eulala Connor
170-171	Stella Ormai
172-173	Eulala Connor
174-175	Eileen Mueller Neill; CHILDCRAFT illustration
176-177	© Brent Jones*
178-179	© Superstock*; CHILDCRAFT photos by Jeff Guerrant
180-181	© Paul Shambroom, Photo Researchers*
182-183	© Jim Sugar, Corbis*; © H. R. Bramaz, Peter Arnold, Inc.*